T0209973

FELT THAT

A Search for Relational Honesty and Truth Amidst Emotional Clutter and Social Chaos

ELAIYNA HOPE

WESTBOW
PRESS®
A DIVISION OF THOMAS NELSON
& ZONDERVAN

WestBow Press books may be ordered through booksellers or by contacting:

WestBow Press
A Division of Thomas Nelson & Zondervan
1663 Liberty Drive
Bloomington, IN 47403
www.westbowpress.com
844-714-3454

Scripture quotations taken from The Holy Bible, English Standard Version® (ESV®) Copyright © 2001 by Crossway, a publishing ministry of Good News Publishers. All rights reserved.

ISBN: 978-1-6642-8486-9 (sc)
ISBN: 978-1-6642-8487-6 (hc)
ISBN: 978-1-6642-8488-3 (e)

Library of Congress Control Number: 2022921846

Print information available on the last page.

WestBow Press rev. date: 05/18/2023

I would like to say a huge thank you to everyone who has helped me along the way:

—My parents, Terry and Jennifer Schwartzkopf, for guiding me through the stories in these pages, teaching me the importance of pursuing Christ, and for always believing in me.

—Braydon, for joining me in shenanigans when I lose my sanity but always helping me get back on track.

—Ashley, for listening to all my rants, doubts, and worries along the way. Thanks for always encouraging me to keep pushing forward.

—To all my family and friends for their support, encouragement, and love.

—And, of course, to those of you who took the time to invest yourself in this journey.

Thank you for giving this book, and me, a chance. I would love nothing more than to see this book touch your lives with the love of the Lord.

Thank you—all of you. You mean the world to me.

INTRODUCTION
A LETTER TO THE READER

Hello, friend!

Though I may not know you in person, I feel as if I am connected to you already. Why? Because you decided to pick up this book, turn to this page, and read. Maybe you liked the cover. Maybe you picked it up by random chance. Or maybe you saw that this book was about the little daily struggles in life—and you related a little too much. You saw that it was meant to inspire women in their spiritual walk and let them know that they aren't alone in their battles. You saw that through this book, someone was seeking to change the narrative of a spiritually independent culture by bringing awareness to universal struggles. It gave you hope that someone out there was advocating for emotional honesty. You saw that this book was written for *you* by someone just like you.

So, yes, I know you—because we are the same. I am thrilled that you are joining me on this voyage of discovering truth through the lens of our Creator. There are many lessons and laughs ahead, but first, let me tell you a little about how this book came to be, who it's for, and how to read it.

The process of creating this book has been quite long and endured many valleys, deserts, and storms. However, it is finally here, and I could not be more thrilled. Take a look back in time with me for just a moment. Let's zoom in on a little girl, no more than seven years old, with blue eyes, blonde pigtails, and a big heart for Jesus. She lived in the country in an old farmhouse, the neighbors' cornfield her backyard.

One day she grabbed her trusty crayons and construction paper and decided to create a devotional for the whole family to read. She spent hours reading her favorite Bible verses and desperately trying to tell a story God would be proud of. Her spelling was off. Her cover design was a little lacking. It was tied together with excessive tape and poorly knotted string. But it was the beginning of a long journey. A journey that you, my friend, are now part of. I have no idea where this path is headed, only that I am supposed to be headed down this path and that He will be walking every step by my side.

I mentioned earlier that this book was written for you. You probably glossed right past that, seeing as that's a common thing for authors to say. However, I am sharing these stories because I know the feeling of loneliness you have battled. Throughout my life, I have had countless girls express loneliness in their search for truth. They have been convinced, through a deceiving and prideful culture, that no one has ever experienced the trials they face. They truly believe that there is no one to ask questions or to relate to. This, my friends, is an abject lie.

In these pages, I have sought to combine scripture with experience to prove that you are not alone. You never have been. I want you to feel completely comfortable being open with yourself and others as you navigate this study. Don't worry though, you're not the only one being vulnerable here. I have shared the good, the bad, and the ugly throughout this book. It is my hope that through my authenticity, you will find the common threads between you and me and our search for a Savior. If even one person can feel His love in the words of this book, then it will have all been worth it.

OK, the last thing before you get to reading is *how* to read this. Normally, this isn't something that would need to be explained. I mean, it's a book … you just *read it*. Yes. But also no. I designed this devotional for group study, but I also wanted to make it functional for individual studies. If you intend to read through this book as a group, I recommend that everyone has their own copy. That way, those involved can scribble in the margins, doodle their favorite verse, or write down prayer requests. Treat this book as a sort of spiritual diary for the time being. Don't be scared to write down your questions or to record a funny comment a friend made. Reading through my old scribbles now, I am reminded of wonderful moments of fellowship, vulnerability, and growth. I guess that is why I want you to have the opportunity to find that same joy, now. If my calculations are correct—fingers crossed— you should be able to meet once a week nearly every week in a semester. Some schools have different amounts of weeks in a school year, so it might not match up perfectly, but I think you get the idea.

To help those who want to lead these discussion groups, I have included questions for your group to talk about afterward. These questions are not supposed to be answered like a test question. They are designed to dig at the heart of your problem, guide you to solutions, and lead you to become open and vulnerable not only with yourself but also with those you are reading this with. The more you invest in this, the more you will benefit from it. That goes for those of you reading individually as well. If you are reading this as an independent study, the pace is up to you. I advise reading at least one a week, but again, it is totally up to you. For both versions, however, make sure to take the time to dissect the discussion questions. These are where you will grow the most. Again, the more you put into this, the more you will get out of it. It's a give-and-take relationship, and you, the reader, are in charge.

One of my deepest desires is that those who read this book find peace in their heart and spiritual inspiration. Please do not

HAPPY AT A STANDSTILL

I took segment one of driver's training in my ninth-grade year and absolutely hated it. In my opinion, the best aspect of driving is usually what most people despise—the stoplight. That glorious red, shining light means I don't have to worry about merging traffic, speed limits, or angry drivers for one blessed moment. I am perfectly happy sitting at a standstill. That way I get to look like I know what I am doing without actually doing anything. It's like a cheat for driving (if you ignore the fact that you still aren't going anywhere, that is).

Driving is a great parallel to the Christian walk. You could probably take any part of a car and turn it into a metaphor for Christianity. But for me, the message that sticks out most clearly is a simple, two-word, declarative statement: "Cars go." That's it—cars go. A car is not created to sit there and look pretty, and neither are we.

Often, when people first accept the Lord as Savior, there is a beautiful fire for the Lord that burns radiantly and illuminates His presence. Unfortunately, as time goes on, the fire seems to fade. For some, their passion is reduced to but an ember. Their fire for the Lord, their burning passion to *go*, is gone. Instead, they live their lives as cars in neutral: avoiding obstacles and dangers by neither moving forward nor backward. It's safe that way, not pressing the gas.

Personally, I don't want to take part in anything that has the potential to disappoint me. I don't want to put myself into vulnerable positions because I know I have been hurt before and could easily be hurt again. This is exactly how some people view their spiritual lives. They are perfectly content sitting still, protected from the potential dangers of disappointment. If you aren't driving, you can't crash. However, we *cannot* live life in park. It just cannot happen. If you never go anywhere, you are never going to get where you want to be. Sometimes, the basic truths are the most important.

In order to progress in our relationship with the Lord, we must actively move in our faith. If we do nothing about our spiritual state, we are never going to change. We have to go in order to get somewhere. We need to reignite that burning passion we once felt and run with it. We need to have an overwhelming desire to *go* again. No more parking or neutral gear. Start running. Don't look back. Don't slow down. God will be right by your side, helping you along your journey. All you need to do is make the decision to switch that gear and *go*.

I know your works: you are neither cold nor hot. Would that you were either cold or hot! So, because you are lukewarm, and neither hot nor cold, I will spit you out of my mouth.
—Revelation 3:15–16 (English Standard Version)

I have chosen the way of faithfulness; I have set my heart on your laws.
—Psalm 119:30 (ESV)

PERSONAL REFLECTION QUESTIONS

- What is a story from your life that is similar to the story shared above? How did it make you feel? How did you react to it?

- When was the last time you were stuck in a spiritual neutral? What did you do to get out of it?

- What could you do on a daily basis to make sure you are pressing the gas pedal in your spiritual life?

- Whom do you have around you to help you stay focused on your growth? If you don't have someone helping you, who could you reach out to (such as family, friends, or pastors)?

- What is your trigger to park? What stops your momentum? Why? What can you do to avoid this?

- What are some things you have learned about yourself and your relationship with God through this story? How can you use this information to help you grow in your faith?

I DON'T NEED A FROG PRINCE

When I turned sixteen, my mom took me to a park to do a birthday photo shoot. We decided on a local garden area, filled with flowers, train tracks, and small streams. It was absolutely beautiful! While walking by one of the streams, I decided to venture to the other side. I carefully jumped from rock to rock, careful to not slip on the shimmery wet spots. After a few moments, my mom called for me to turn around. I had unintentionally created a great photo opportunity and my mom was not about it miss it. Laughing, I turned to give her a big, cheesy smile but was suddenly very distracted. Something had just touched my foot. I looked down quickly to determine what it could have been and was delighted when I laid eyes on the adorable culprit. It was a little, light green frog—smaller than the tip of my thumb.

I gently picked it up and showed it to my mom, laughing, as I pretended to kiss it. "Maybe it's my true love," I joked. "My prince in disguise!"

My mom, ever the photographer, snapped a great picture of me almost kissing the frog. It makes me laugh every time I see it. I knew the frog wouldn't turn into a lovely, handsome prince, but it was fun to pretend.

I don't know about you, but I find the idea of relationships utterly terrifying—not bad, but scary nonetheless. It's hard to find a guy who loves the Lord, takes care of your heart, and fits your personality. I'm sure you've had your own experiences surrounding this, too. It almost seems like it would be easier to accidentally find a frog prince!

Society tells us that without a significant other, we are sad or lonely, or something is wrong with us. However, sometimes the pursuit of a partner leads us to a worse state than we began. We begin to psychoanalyze ourselves and pick out every physical, mental, or emotional flaw. We obsess about how to remedy our situation, turning to things like makeup or intelligence to try to make ourselves more appealing. However, this doesn't work. Instead of "fixing" yourself you have created an endless cycle of self-hatred and a complete lack of confidence. In the pursuit to become "happy" through a significant other, we lose track of where our real happiness comes from. We make ourselves miserable trying to fulfill every unattainable standard the world has set. Our culture's definition of happy has led millions away from it. I speak for the masses when I say it has become nearly impossible to find any source of relational peace—especially at this phase in our lives.

The world, unfortunately, is a very messed-up place. Though they tell you that consistent happiness is only found through love, you cannot bend to believe these lies. Love is, of course, a blessing from God and something that should be celebrated when pursued in the right manner. However, the only thing that will always be consistent is God's love for you. The way the world tells you to find happiness isn't going to work. It is a plain, simple truth. What they suggest may be great temporarily, but it will eventually lead to more sadness and loneliness than you had ever imagined. The world's rules and expectations are eternally inconsistent. Every lie the world tells you, self-negative thought, and fearful doubt of the future is seen by Him. He knows what you are going through, but more importantly, He knows how to make you feel whole. He is always with you, fighting for your peace, happiness, and security in Him. Don't become distracted by the world's inconsistencies and expectations.

I might not know much, but I do know that you don't need a frog prince. You may eventually be blessed with a partner who will love and take care of you, but your focus should be on the never-failing truths of God first. He is the only constant. If you put your faith or hope in anything else, you are in for a huge disappointment. We are flawed, fallible human beings. We are not going to get it right every time. In fact, we are probably going to get it *wrong* quite often. However, we can count on the fact that He always brings us back to Him, leading us on the path He has personally prepared. His eternal, unchanging love comes before anything this fickle world could offer.

May the God of hope fill you with all joy and peace as you trust in him, so that you may overflow with hope by the power of the Holy Spirit.
—2 Chronicles 15:4 (ESV)

Jesus Christ is the same yesterday and today and forever.
—Hebrews 13:8 (ESV)

Every good and perfect gift is from above, coming down from the Father of the heavenly lights, who does not change like shifting shadows.
—James 1:17 (ESV)

PERSONAL REFLECTION QUESTIONS

> What is a story from your life that is similar to the story shared above? How did it make you feel? How did you react to it?

> Do you get lost in life sometimes? Is that because you have started taking directions from yourself? Why? What can you do to shift your navigation back toward Christ?

> Have you experienced some hardships in relationships? Have these led you closer to fellowship with God or further away? Why? What can you do to help those situations draw you closer to Him?

> Do you struggle to remember that you are God's *chosen* child? Spend some time researching scripture on this topic. Write down some verses that help you remember that you are His child. Try reading these through every morning, and record how this changes your perspectives and thoughts throughout the day. *(Some personal favorites include Galatians 3:25-26, Romans 8:13-14, and John 1:12-13)*

> Do you feel pressure to be in a relationship right now? Do you think you are ready for one? Why or why not? Have you prayed about the situation, or are you acting merely on your desires? Write down any areas you might be struggling with and pray about them.

> What are some things you have learned about yourself and your relationship with God through this story? How can you use this information to help you grow in your faith?

I DIDN'T TOUCH IT

Basketball season is finally here and you can practically feel the tension in the air. The first game in the big tournament is this week. Coupled with the general anxiety that accompanies an athletic competition, there is enormous pressure on your team to win—not just because your team is good but because you have history. Your team has won the state tournament for the past *four years*. Your school, your friends, and your city are expecting big things.

After an exhausting first half of practice, your coach finally breaks for water. You walk over and grab your bottle. Just as it touches your lips, but before you get any water, the captain of the team walks over. "Hey, girlie, that's my water bottle! Whatcha doing?" she says, laughing.

Humiliated (because this isn't the first time this has happened), you yank it away from your mouth, wipe the top off, and quickly say, "I didn't touch it!"

She looks at you, confused. "You did too. I saw it touch your lips."

"No, I didn't! I stopped right beforehand. I didn't touch it."

"Yeah … OK. Just be careful next time. I'm putting mine over here—don't touch it."

Humiliation courses through your whole body. Why in the world would you lie about a *water bottle*? What made you do it? It stays on your mind all night and through to the next day. The pressure of doing well in the tournament mixed with the pressure to impress the captain got the better of you. You lied to avoid creating confrontation. Instead, you created mortification. You failed your teammate. You failed yourself. Ultimately, you failed God.

Social pressure is one of the strongest and most manipulative forces on the planet. The most secure people fracture under its touch. The smartest are fooled and the kindest are left selfish. People can turn on the flip of a dime simply because of fear of negative perception. It's a complicated business. No one wants their good reputation marred.

Not surprisingly, the Bible teaches the exact opposite approach. While society teaches us to bend the truth for ease, God calls us to stay on the straight and narrow no matter the consequences. The truth never claimed to be easy. However, He doesn't leave us to deal with our difficulties alone. He desires to aid us in our pursuit of truth and calls us to rely on His power. It is His strength that fortifies us and reinforces our ability to fight the pressures of the world. He will help you to not bend under the weight of others' perceived expectations. Don't compromise yourself or your faith, especially over something juvenile like a water bottle. Next time you face the temptation to give in, remember that Christ can give you the power to overcome. It will take time; you won't win every trial. But the more you practice, the more you will succeed with His strength. Soon, the decisions will become easier. You won't even have to think about what the right decision is because you will know in your soul what you are supposed to do. Open your ears and heart to the truths of the Spirit. They will never let you down.

If the world hates you, keep in mind that it hated me first.
—John 15:18 (ESV)

Am I now trying to win the approval of human beings, or of God? Or am I trying to please people? If I were still trying to please people, I would not be a servant of Christ.
—Galatians 1:10 (ESV)

PERSONAL REFLECTION QUESTIONS

- ➤ What is a story from your life that is similar to the story shared above? How did it make you feel? How did you react to it?
- ➤ Why do you think it is our natural inclination to lie, even though deep down we know it is pointless? What can we do to fix that?
- ➤ Is there a situation like this right now in your life that you are avoiding addressing? Remember that though white lies are often the most embarrassing to apologize for, they are just as important to mend.
- ➤ Why do *you* bend to peer pressure?
- ➤ Do you easily give up when peer pressure comes, or do you fight against it? Why or why not?
- ➤ What are some things you have learned about yourself and your relationship with God through this story? How can you use this information to help you grow in your faith?

A SCREECHING HALT

March 7, 2019, is the day that changed the course of one of my best friends' lives. It is a day I still recall often, thanking God for His protection every time. It was a cold but slightly frantic morning in her household. There were lunches to be made, quizzes and tests to prepare for, along with all the other morning-routine stressors that accompany high school. They were a bit behind schedule when her brother pulled out of the driveway to take them to school, which only added to the chaos. It was the perfect storm. He and the other driver headed towards him were so distracted they didn't realize the collision was about to incur until it was too late. Computers, purses, and people were thrown violently as the car somersaulted into the ditch. Then, everything went dark.

She awoke to an intense pain in her chest and felt her younger sister trying helplessly to get her out of the car. Turning to check on her brother, she felt her breath catch. Something was clearly very wrong. With what little strength she had, she attempted to get him out of the car—it was no use. They quickly called 911. All she could do was wait until someone came to help them. Alone, hurt, and freezing, she sat on the curb and sobbed on a cold, bitter Michigan day—the day her whole life came to a screeching halt.

My friend and her little sister spent a few days in the hospital—they had some significant injuries, but thankfully nothing life-altering. Her brother, on the other hand, was a different story. For a while, we questioned whether he was going to make it or not. It was a terrifying time for this family.

I'm not sure how you respond in situations like this. Hopefully, you haven't had to encounter this in your own life. However, our broken world would suggest otherwise. When I was informed of this situation, I immediately dropped everything and ran to help. I don't mean figuratively, either. I dropped my notebooks and ran out of the classroom to go call my mom. I was going to go help *immediately*.

In the first stages of this event, I was asked to be pretty hands-on with helping their family. As time went on, they slowly made progress toward healing and required less help. However, I was finding it difficult to pull back. Instead of slowly weaning myself off, I dove even deeper into their problems. I got my hands on everything I could, doing anything possible to fix *something*. As I am sure you could guess, this approach of desperation didn't work well. In fact, absolutely no one benefitted from it. I didn't help them or myself. Instead, I self-sabotaged by plaguing myself with stress and anxiety. I served my fear and pride instead of their family. It took over my life, affecting everything I did. Not only was I failing to help them, but I was failing to handle the bumps in my own life. Don't get me wrong; you should always support your friends and seek to help where you can. However, I was far too emotionally and mentally involved. I had tried to take God's role as Healer. Let me tell you something, it doesn't work well when you try to fill God's shoes.

Eventually, I hit my breaking point and was forced to my knees. I cried out to God, begging Him to help me release the situation into His hands. It was then that *I* began the process of healing. It takes a while to learn how to release control into the hands of another, even if the other person is God. By His grace, I was eventually able to come to a healthy relationship with their situation. I slowly saw my anxiety begin to lessen and joy sneak back into my days. It was a bit of a long road, but one that I am glad to have taken. Some of the most important life lessons are not learned in a split second, but rather require time to develop and comprehend. I learned that despite how much you may desire to fix all the problems in your world, you do not have the strength to do so. Some tasks are not meant for our solving. They are intended for the Creator. We cannot possibly handle situations of that enormity.

We have no strength in ourselves. Though we may rightly desire to help others, we must always remind ourselves that it is Christ who is the Great Physician—not us. There are some tasks not meant for us to handle. They are intended for the Creator. However, if you are being crushed by a weight that was not yours to carry, know that there is relief. Talk to Him about your struggles. Explain to Him why it is so difficult. Have a conversation with Him. Open your heart to hear from Him. He does speak, but we must be willing to listen and receive. Take a long, deep breath. You do the most good by letting God do His job.

> *Do not be anxious about anything, but in every situation, by prayer and petition, with thanksgiving, present your requests to God. And the peace of God, which transcends all understanding, will guard your hearts and your minds in Christ Jesus.*
> —Philippians 4:6–7 (ESV)

PERSONAL REFLECTION QUESTIONS

- What is a story from your life that is similar to the story shared above? How did it make you feel? How did you react to it?
- Do you have a fix-it personality, or do you struggle to put in effort when it doesn't directly affect you? Why or why not?
- Why do you struggle to give God the reins in hard situations?
- We know we cannot fix the things in life by ourselves, yet we still try. Why do you think that is? What can you do to start changing your mindset in life?
- What keeps you from letting go?
- What are some things you have learned about yourself and your relationship with God through this story? How can you use this information to help you grow in your faith?

GOOD ENOUGH?

One thing you should know about me is that I tend to be *very* stubborn. Sometimes that fact works in my favor. Other times it leaves me exhausted, brain-numb, and irritated. My stubbornness decided to try to get the better of me one day in high school as I was studying for a test. A test for what? Well, this happened to be the largest logic test we would have all year.

Traditional logic, with all its terms, processes, and proofs, did not click easily with me. Some people seemed to grasp the material immediately, which infuriated me even more. Because others learned so easily, I felt like I had no excuse to not succeed. If other people could do it, I was positive I could as well. However, that confidence quickly dwindled when I looked at the clock. It was two in the morning, which meant my test was in about eight hours and I was in no position to get a passing grade. There was absolutely nothing I could do but sit back and watch the misery unfold. It didn't matter how stubborn or determined I was, this concept was not sticking. I'd done my best, but I was pretty sure that wasn't enough.

Is anyone else out there a committed perfectionist? Obsessed with being in the top ranks? Addicted to having different talents? First off, let's be clear: it isn't bad to love perfection. It isn't bad to want to be good at what you do. However, it *is* bad to let them have such a hold over you that they begin to ruin your quality of life. Your hobbies should be just that—hobbies. Your desire for perfection should never lead to the intentional or unintentional abuse of your body or mind. God wants you to do well and give your best effort, but He does not expect you to destroy your quality of life over a logic test. We are fallible, fallen creatures. We are incapable of perfection, and He knows that. We can try to get as close as possible, but it is never going to be enough. That is why we need a Savior. He knows we desire perfection but cannot attain it. When we connect the achievement of perfection with our self-worth, we have given ourselves an impossible standard. It is impossible to attain, therefore leading to complete mental anguish. God does not view our worth on account of our perfection. Neither should you.

Not only is perfectionism a dangerous and toxic mindset for you, but it is also dangerous for those around you. If you approach your life obsessed with attaining perfection, others will feel as if they should do the same. Perfectionism is a silent and deadly virus. It often takes hold before you even notice its existence. Having unrealistic expectations of yourself or others will inevitably lead to a negative spiral in mental, physical, and spiritual health. It may seem like having perfectionist tendencies has been a benefit, but I promise you that the consequences far outweigh any meager benefit you may find. It preaches lies to your heart that you have no worth if you are not perfect. This is a thought that cannot even be entertained. Your worth as a person is not defined by what you can accomplish. The truth is, God wants you for you. He doesn't care if you aren't the best. He specifically designed you to function *exactly the way you are.* Yes, we make mistakes. Yes, it is always good to improve! However, we cannot fixate on improvement so much that we replace our identity in Christ with an identity in perfection. Our mistakes shouldn't make us miserable. Instead, they should open our eyes to our need for salvation.

It is hard when you know that you could've done better.

However, this does not mean you are a failure. Your identity is in God, the perfect Savior of the world. It is so much better to rely on His true perfection than our biased, warped, earthly version. You, my friend, are not defined by your accomplishments but by the grace and love of the Father. The acceptance and belief of that is the start of the journey toward the life God has planned for you.

But he said to me, "My grace is sufficient for you, for my power is made perfect in weakness." Therefore I will boast all the more gladly about my weaknesses, so that Christ's power may rest on me. That is why, for Christ's sake, I delight in weaknesses, in insults, in hardships, in persecutions, in difficulties. For when I am weak, then I am strong."
—2 Corinthians 12:9–10 (ESV)

PERSONAL REFLECTION QUESTIONS

- What is a story from your life that is similar to the story shared above? How did it make you feel? How did you react to it?
- What areas in life are you a perfectionist in? Is this a healthy relationship you have with this activity, or has it turned into a personal measurement of your worth? Why?
- Do you have trouble placing your value in Christ rather than in your abilities? Remember that these abilities are meant to bring glory back to Him! Is that how you are using them?
- What do you do when you catch yourself misplacing your identity? Research some verses on this topic and write down the one that speaks the most to you. Next time you catch

yourself, repeat this verse to yourself as a reminder and encouragement.

- ➤ Do you have an accountability partner? They are great tools to keep you focused on the Lord. Who do you have in your life that you could talk to about this?
- ➤ What are some things you have learned about yourself and your relationship with God through this story? How can you use this information to help you grow in your faith?

Q-U-I-T-T-E-R

"Dad, you *know* what I am trying to say. You know what I mean" I laughed. I knew he was just messing with me. It was funny—I deserved to be poked at. "Dad, seriously. I quit." I said, laughing as I walked away.

"Oh, so you're a quitter now, huh? Q-U-I-T-T-E-R!"

For some reason, this comment struck a nerve. I wasn't sure why, so I tried to ignore it. But the more he repeated it, the more it bothered me. Tears sprung to my eyes and my hands started shaking. I knew it was a joke and even thought it was funny, so why was I responding like this? I walked back into the room with a lump in my throat. I choked out a "goodnight" and left, hurt and confused.

I am probably just tired, I told myself. *You just need to go to bed. Don't make a big deal out of this.* I knew he didn't mean anything by his little chant, but it resonated deeply. Being called a quitter was not a small thing. Quitting means that you gave up on everyone who was depending on you, leaving them to fend for themselves. It means you thought of no one but yourself. How could someone accuse me of that—even jokingly?

As I stared out my window contemplating this question, I came to a strange conclusion. Though it wasn't my dad's intent to make me contemplate this thought, his comment held more truth than I cared to admit. I realized I had quit on someone recently. I had quit on God. When things had gotten difficult, I didn't fight to preserve my relationship with Him. Instead, I took the easy route. I was tired, so I became complacent. I had decided to quit giving my energy to God so that I could focus more on what I thought was important. And after taking a moment to evaluate how my life was going, it was clear that my priorities were not in line with God's. I was long overdue for a spiritual makeover. This time, God was going to lead every step of the way.

Complacency in the faith is extremely dangerous, and unfortunately, it is also extremely common. We all love an easy life. However, what God calls us to do is not easy. That hardship often results in internal friction. We become angry that our path doesn't seem as easy as others we see. We fight against Him, believing that He must have chosen wrong. My friends, God didn't choose the wrong path for you. You are right where you are supposed to be. However, it is up to you to not give up on walking down the road He has laid out.

God deserves your energy. Don't quit on His will for you. I know it is hard. I know you are tired and weary. However, I also know that He is going to be the one to fill you. He will heal you, encourage you, and set you on the right path. Taking your own path is tempting. I get it. The grass looks greener, and the path looks shorter … it is quite enticing, but don't give in to the lies of ease. He is worth the effort. Fight for Him the way He is fighting for you.

> *The righteous person may have many troubles, but the Lord delivers him from them all.*
> —Psalm 34:19 (ESV)
>
> *Whatever you do, work at it with all your heart, as working for the Lord, not for human masters.*
> —Colossians 3:23 (ESV)

PERSONAL REFLECTION QUESTIONS

- What is a story from your life that is similar to the story shared above? How did it make you feel? How did you react to it?
- Is there anything in your life that is taking away from the pursuit of your relationship with God? What can you do about that?
- Is there something you were working toward in your spiritual life that you quit on? What caused you to quit it? What can you do to start again?
- Take a bird's-eye view of your life. What things do you notice that are surprising? Are they good or bad? Why?
- Are there any areas of your life you notice yourself trying to control? Is there something you feel called to quit?
- What are some things you have learned about yourself and your relationship with God through this story? How can you use this information to help you grow in your faith?

INFECTIOUS OBSESSION

Social media is infectious. I know that isn't a novel revelation, but it is one that I think we tend to forget about quite often. It isn't that we are trying to become attached to social media … it just kind of happens. It begins as an innocent way to stay connected with long-lost or distant friends, but as time goes on it slowly eats up more time. Next thing you know, hours have passed without accomplishing anything of significance. Instead of merely using your device as a communication tool, it has become a time waster and an addicting entertainment device.

However, it does not just entertain us. Social media is brimming with messages the world is trying to implant into our minds. They take hold of our psychology, using specific tactics to get us to believe that we must act, look, or be a certain way. We often don't even realize the constant comparisons we subject ourselves to. However, the toxic messages that we have become subject to affect us in nearly every aspect of our lives. It begins by subconsciously changing our habits of thought. Then, slowly, those thoughts begin to affect our actions. We mold our behaviors to reflect those portrayed to us. We begin to constantly reassess ourselves to determine if we can "fit in" to the culture we see. To put it in blunt terms, we are constantly making changes to ourselves so that we can satisfy the desires of a sin-based culture. When it is phrased like that, it sounds repulsive. However, I would be the first to admit to being fooled. I have faced many internal battles related to image, intelligence, and recognition. These messages the world sends are veiled, appearing helpful or beautiful to the untrained eye. But it is up to us to uncover the poisonous subliminal messages of the world, checking their reflection in the mirror of God's truth. We have unknowingly altered almost every aspect of our lives because of the lies we have been told. It is time to strip ourselves of these lies and form our identity around the *real* truth.

Don't get me wrong here. I am not saying that social media is inherently bad—simply that we must be careful. Why? Because we as a culture have bought into the idea that to be accepted, we must be like everyone else. We must fit that perfect mold that is constantly advertised to us. It seems as if authenticity and cultural likeability have become opposite realities.

No one desires to be an outcast, so we make the changes that culture requires of us—often without a second thought. How often, though, do we change that quickly to fit *God's* standards for our lives?

We are quick to change for public perception but slow to change for spiritual benefit. We have an awful habit of ignoring God when He speaks to us, then claiming that He doesn't speak. Why? Because the changes He wants from us aren't always fun. Sometimes they require work that we don't want to do. It requires much more discipline to make the changes God wants than the changes the world wants.

Though following God's path is harder in the beginning, it leads to an ending more beautiful than we can imagine. He desires for us to rest in His love, peace, and mercy. We can only receive those blessings, however, if we listen to Him when He speaks. Guard your heart and train your eyes to see the truth. His truth will always set you free.

Do not be conformed to this world, but continuously be transformed by the renewing of your minds so that you may be able to determine what God's will is—what is proper, pleasing, and perfect.
—Romans 12:2 (ESV)

Do not merely listen to the word, and so deceive yourselves. Do what it says.
—James 1:22 (ESV)

How can a young person stay on the path of purity? By living according to your word.
—Psalm 119:9 (ESV)

PERSONAL REFLECTION QUESTIONS

> What is a story from your life that is similar to the story shared above? How did it make you feel? How did you react to it?

> Check your phone stats. How much time did you spend on social media so far this week? Was your time spent on social media connecting personally with friends, or looking at fake snapshots of other people's lives? Do you think this is healthy?

> Have you changed anything about yourself to make other people like you more? Do you think this is a good motivation to change yourself? Why or why not? What is a good reason to make changes to your personality or appearance?

- Do the social norms you see in society come from a spiritually sound place or our fallen natures? Why do you think we try to copy them if we know they aren't scripturally sound?
- What is something you could do to push a new social norm that is scripturally sound? How can you push back against the lies being shared on social media?
- What are some things you have learned about yourself and your relationship with God through this story? How can you use this information to help you grow in your faith?

REDEFINING ROUTINE

Morning routines are incredibly important. They can make or break your entire day. Personally, if I am thrown out of rhythm even the smallest bit, my entire day feels off-kilter. When I was in high school, I had a specific routine. I got up at the same time every morning, put on my outfit, did my hair and makeup, then went downstairs for breakfast and coffee with my mom. Spending time in the morning with my mom is one of my fondest memories of high school. It was early enough in the morning that the raucous of life hadn't picked up yet, but we were still awake. It was as if we were stealing our own quiet time to converse with each other. Sometimes, we didn't even say anything. We just sat together and drank our coffee in quiet, peaceful bliss. Other times, we laughed so hard we woke up my dad and brother! The mornings were whatever we needed them to be. They were perfect. I miss them a lot, now.

Sometimes, when I would have a test or a quiz, I would have to spend my morning studying instead of with my mom. Though it was better for my academics, the rest of my day just felt *wrong* somehow. My soul experienced unrest. Because I didn't prepare myself for the day ahead, it drained me. I was irritable, exhausted, and anxious. The bad days helped shed light on the importance of emotional and spiritual preparation.

How we begin our day can have massive effects on its quality. I've spoken to many of my classmates, and it was a little concerning to hear their morning routine. Why? Because it consisted of checking their phone, throwing on an outfit, and rushing out the door to class. There was no semblance of rest in their routine. There was also not a single mention of spending time with God. Yet, we wonder why we are overwhelmed and anxious all the time. It is time we fight to redefine routine.

If something as small as having a quiet cup of coffee in the morning can change the trajectory of your day, how much more could we benefit from spending quiet time with God? I know … you're tired, you aren't fully awake yet, you're going to be late … I've heard (and made) all these excuses before. It took me almost twenty years to establish a morning routine that consistently included spending time with God. In fact, let me be brutally honest with you for a minute. Morning devotionals are an absolute struggle for me. That's completely ironic, seeing as I write them (I don't know; don't ask me to explain that. I've got nothing). But it's true! I passionately dislike early mornings. The idea of trying to learn deep, spiritual material at six in the morning sounds awful to me. However, that isn't what your time with God needs to be.

Morning devotionals do not need to consist of deep spiritual study. Instead, they may simply be a time of prayer or meditation. They may differ from morning to morning, depending on what your soul needs that day. Just like how my mom and I spanned from silence to laughter, your time with God can span from study to silence. Sometimes, just sitting in quiet communion with Him is exactly what you need. It truly doesn't matter what you do in your time with God, as long as you are giving Him some of that time. That is your time to let Him fill you up and prepare you for the day ahead, whatever way you need that morning.

Don't cheat yourself out of peace. I know the extra ten minutes of sleep is tempting. I've given into that trap quite a few times, myself. However, it is nothing compared to the rest you find in the Father. You have control over the trajectory of your day. Things may still go wrong. You may still be tired or anxious. However, you will be experiencing those hardships with the knowledge and belief that He is walking with you. Spend your mornings sipping a cup of coffee with Jesus. I promise you won't regret it.

> *Do not be anxious about anything, but in everything by prayer and supplication with thanksgiving let your requests be made known to God. And the peace of God, which surpasses all understanding, will guard your hearts and your minds in Christ Jesus.*
> —Philippians 4:6–7 (ESV)

PERSONAL REFLECTION QUESTIONS

> What is a story from your life that is similar to the story shared above? How did it make you feel? How did you react to it?

> What is the largest factor that prohibits you from following through on quiet time with Jesus? What can you do to change this?

> When you do devotionals, do you do them in the morning or at night? What are the benefits or detriments of doing it at that time? What benefits could come from switching the time? Would that help you to stay more focused?

> Is there a worship song, verse, or story you could read that would set your mood for the day? Create a list of

Scripture-related things that make you happy and try reading/listening/watching one each morning.

> As you redefine your routine, keep a journal of your progress. What have you found has become easier in your day? Are you reminded of certain Scriptures more often? Keep notes!

> What are some things you have learned about yourself and your relationship with God through this story? How can you use this information to help you grow in your faith?

CAN'T MAKE THE SHOT

When I say that the end of my sophomore year of basketball was quite eventful, I mean it. One of our starters completely tore her ACL and was out for the season. Another starter had her head purposefully smashed against an opponent's knee, causing her to black out. This resulted in an immediate trip to the ER, where she found she had suffered a severe concussion and would not be allowed to play the rest of the season. Someone else on the team broke her finger during practice and required surgery, while another broke her wrist and was out for the season. We were dropping like flies. It was absolute chaos, and I was in the middle of it all. Why? Because this fiasco resulted in my becoming a starter. Ideally, I would have been a starter because I earned it … but desperate times call for desperate measures. The pressure was crushing. My team had a legacy. We had won the state title four years in a row and were expected to take the title again. It was going to be tough with our small team, but we were ready to fight. When injury after injury struck, the whole team was left scrambling.

If I am honest, when I was told I was going to be a starter, I didn't believe it. I thought it was a joke. How could it be real? I was a first-time varsity player—a bench warmer! The past few games I had even been doing *worse* than normal. I couldn't seem to make a single shot, defend without fouling, or even pass without a turnover. I was a wreck, constantly reprimanding myself because I couldn't do anything right. In my first two games as a starter, I didn't score a single point. The next thing I knew, I found myself on the bench fighting back tears. How could I be such a failure? How could I let my team down like this?

As I sat there trying to figure out where I went wrong, one of the coaches came and sat next to me.

I already knew what she was going to say. "Be tough. Fight for the rebounds. Look for the open shots. Drive!" Yeah, I'd heard it all before. I didn't need to be told again.

I looked up at her, prepared for the talk.

When I met her eyes, they were full of concern. "Hey. What's up? Are you all right?"

I didn't even know what to say. This was not going the way I expected it. "Yeah … I guess so. I don't know what I'm doing wrong out there. I'm in a slump, and I don't know how to get out and help my team the way everyone is expecting. I'm failing everyone and don't know what to do to fix it."

I had expected an agreement here. I fully anticipated her telling me I was right in my assessment and that I needed to figure it out as soon as possible. But she didn't. She just looked at me and softly smiled. "I know what's wrong. You don't believe in yourself. After everything went down with this team, you've put so much pressure on yourself that you are drowning. But I know you can do it. I have seen you. You *are* a beast out there, but only when you trust yourself. Ignore the pressure. You do what you can do. That open lane? I know you see it. I know you want to go in. So why don't you? Because you are afraid. Don't be. You drive in that lane and show that team who's in control. Hear me? Now go get back in that game."

After the initial shock wore off, I headed over to get subbed in. I went back in the game with four fouls and three minutes left on the clock. It felt different, though. I felt that I could do it again. Keep in mind, I didn't magically start playing better. I didn't make the game-winning shot, become a beast at defense, or clean up every board. What did change, however, was my attitude about my performance. Instead of being upset and hard on myself, I noticed and celebrated small improvements. I started to see some of the things I was doing right, instead of just what I was doing wrong. I was even able to start cheering for those that *were* doing a great job! That perspective shift continued into future practices, eventually leading to some fantastic games. She may not have known it at the time, but my coach gave me exactly what I needed to beat my slump.

Have you ever been in a spiritual slump? A time when you just can't make the right decision no matter how hard you try? I know I have. Maybe you are in one right now. It feels like nothing you do is good enough. No progress is notable. Even when you try to help, you only hinder others. It can be extremely discouraging. It is so easy to believe that you are on your own in your spiritual journey. Don't believe that lie. Look for those who are reaching out to you. You are never truly alone when you are God's child. Who has come to sit next to you to encourage you? Is there someone in your life who might be able to guide you to the answers? Those people are your key to success. When you are feeling down and out, lean on them. That's what they're there for. It is OK to require their strength for a while. Ask them for guidance and use their wisdom to better yourself. Someone will always come around to point you back to your Creator.

Sometimes it is hard to get that perspective shift. It exposes the things you are doing wrong, which often hurts. However, you can't improve if you don't know where there is room for growth. Notice the little victories throughout your day. Celebrate improvements, no matter how small they are! The knowledge that you are growing closer to God will only encourage you to continue working hard at it. You must lean on God and others; your strength alone is not enough. He will get you out of your slump one little victory at a time.

> *Do you not know that in a race all the runners run, but only one gets the prize? Run in such a way as to get the prize.*
> —1 Corinthians 9:24 (ESV)
>
> *We are hard pressed on every side, but not crushed; perplexed, but not in despair; persecuted, but not abandoned; struck down, but not destroyed.*
> —2 Corinthians 4:8–9 (ESV)

PERSONAL REFLECTION QUESTIONS

➤ What is a story from your life that is similar to the story shared above? How did it make you feel? How did you react to it?

➤ Spiritual slumps are tough. Sometimes you don't even notice you are in one until you realize just how different things have been lately. Take a second to evaluate yourself. Where are you right now? What can you do to get even closer to God?

➤ Identify three people in your life that can "coach" you as you work on getting closer to God. Next time you notice yourself in a slump, reach out to these people and ask them for guidance.

- Once you know you're in a spiritual slump, what methods do you use to draw yourself back to what matters? What does scripture say about this topic?
- What little victories have you noticed about yourself this week? Celebrate and pray over these. Ask God to help these little victories continue to grow into larger-scale ones.
- What are some things you have learned about yourself and your relationship with God through this story? How can you use this information to help you grow in your faith?

LITTLE TOO LATE

I'd been ready to move to college since I was in middle school. I wanted to study my passions, not the standard classes we were all forced to take. It seemed like a waste of time. So, when I finally got to college, I went full force into my studies. In my first semester of college, I was enrolled in over twenty credits. I was determined to not quit any of the classes. Because of that, I became a slave to work. I barely slept, never rested, and certainly never had time to manage a social life. I would watch people on the sidewalk laughing with their new friends, taking pictures, or going to events together. I didn't have anything even close to that. I was alone. I had some fantastic grades, great standing with my professors, and many academic successes to be proud of—but I had completely forgotten about the need for companionship. Sure, I wanted friends, but I didn't create time for them. I slowly started to bring myself to a more normal schedule as time went on. By the time I was ready for new friendships, everyone else had moved past that stage. Most people had already formed their friend groups and weren't looking to make new friends. They were focused on the budding relationships they had already been cultivating. I had chosen accolades over friendship. It was time to pay the price. I don't regret being focused on my future. However, looking back, I realize I didn't have to choose between friends or accolades. I could've chosen friends *and* accolades. I learned this a little too late.

Sometimes, Christians can fall into this trap in their faith. We focus on doing good things, obeying the rules, having a good reputation, and serving others. In the mad rush to make people know we are Christians by our actions, we forget about developing relationships—specifically our relationship with God. We say, "Look, God, at all these *things* I am doing for you!" while we invest no time in our personal relationship with Him. We do not take time alone with Him. The private, intimate moments of revealing your heart are shoved to the side so that we can be showy for others. We fall into the belief system that we need to give people reasons to like us, or that we must convince God to love us. Our desperate attempt to earn love has in turn taken our attention away from formulating that very relationship. Now, we are left with nothing but regret.

Don't realize this too late. Don't lose track of what is important. He doesn't need you to give Him reasons to love you. He gave the ultimate sacrifice of love for you before you even existed. He loves you more than you could possibly understand. Your attempts to convince Him are futile. Don't waste your time. In truth, we *can't* ever prove ourselves to Him. We are naturally sinful and completely depraved. We are completely undeserving of God's love, yet He loves us more fully than we will ever be able to comprehend. Focus on investing yourself into that love, not into momentary success. He wants a relationship with you. He is waiting every day for you to get to know Him better. A relationship with Him is the most wonderful thing you could ever accomplish. Focus on the heart. From there, everything will change.

You will seek me and find me when you seek me with all your heart.
—Jeremiah 29:13 (ESV)

Am I now trying to win the approval of human beings, or of God? Or am I trying to please people? If I were still trying to please people, I would not be a servant of Christ.
—Galatians 1:10 (ESV)

PERSONAL REFLECTION QUESTIONS

- What is a story from your life that is similar to the story shared above? How did it make you feel? How did you react to it?
- Are you stuck trying to give people reasons to like you instead of showing them your true personality? Why? What can you do to become more authentic with others and your relationship with Christ?
- Why do you struggle with believing people would like you for who you are? Have you placed your identity in people's opinions of you rather than the opinion of God? He tells us that we are loved, treasured, and cared for.
- What can you work on this week to solidify and strengthen your identity placement?
- Spend some time in your Bible researching what it tells you about yourself and your identity in Christ. Which verses stick out to you? Write down some encouraging verses and refer back to them when you find your identity placement shifting.
- What are some things you have learned about yourself and your relationship with God through this story? How can you use this information to help you grow in your faith?

IN THE MOMENT

There are places, people, and things in life that never fail to remind you of moments you would rather forget. Sometimes I am successful in forgetting and ignoring those undesirable times, but other days the weight pulls me down. It isn't that you *want* to think about it or be sad, but sometimes you just can't get it off your mind. It seems like it should be easy. People are always full of advice, telling you to "choose to be happy", "ignore the bad stuff", or "keep your perspective". It's like they think that you pray one time and God will take it all away in one powerful snap. Problem solved. It would be lovely if that were the case. However, it isn't quite how that works.

We live in a world that only advertises perfection. When perfection is our only comparison, it is easy to feel like we must hide our "undesirable" emotions or problems from others. After all, the best people are only ever happy, healthy, and enjoying their life, right? It is a toxic mindset that nearly everyone I know has adopted to some degree—including myself. Perfectionism is a worldwide epidemic—and it is leading to our demise.

It isn't healthy to pretend that everything in life is perfect. To pretend that our life is perfect is to pretend that we are not mortal. It is to pretend that we are not how God created us. He didn't design us to be perfect. You haven't done anything wrong by experiencing emotional or physical struggle. It is part of our lot in life. We must accept that fact if we are to gain the proper perspective of our undesirable moments. I promise you that there are going to be moments in your life that are horrible. You've probably already experienced some of them. While it is not healthy to dwell on these times in excess, it is also not healthy to ignore them. God wants to use those times of struggle to bring you closer to Him. If you ignore it and pretend all is fine, you are robbing yourself of a closer relationship with Him. You are denying yourself the opportunity to grow in faith and trust. Every moment holds potential for growth.

He knows you aren't perfect—He loves you anyways. It is through your imperfections, the cracks in your soul, that He can shine His light. Cling to His love and hope. When sadness threatens to blur your vision, look for His clarity. My friend, you aren't wrong for struggling. Share your heart with Him, learn to understand your struggles, and use that understanding to grow with others. That is how you get through. God is giving you each day as a gift, each moment as a reminder of His love and care for you, and each breath to remind you that *you are still breathing.* You aren't defeated, so keep going. He's going to put you back together piece by piece. When He does, you can share your story of redemption with others who are in the same spot you once were. It is a beautiful thing to share your brokenness. Share it with peace and joy, knowing He is holding you in His mighty hands. He's got you.

But he said to me, "My grace is sufficient for you, for my power is made perfect in weakness." Therefore I will boast all the more gladly of my weaknesses, so that the power of Christ may rest upon me. For the sake of Christ, then, I am content with weaknesses, insults, hardships, persecutions, and calamities. For when I am weak, then I am strong.
—2 Corinthians 12:9-10 (ESV)

> *Surely there is not a righteous man on earth who does good and never sins.*
> —Ecclesiastes 7:20 (ESV)

> *If we say we have no sin, we deceive ourselves, and the truth is not in us.*
> —1 John 1:8 (ESV)

PERSONAL REFLECTION QUESTIONS

- What is a story from your life that is similar to the story shared above? How did it make you feel? How did you react to it?
- Are you in a series of hard times right now, or are you at a resting point? What do you think your next steps should be to keep moving?
- Do you struggle with the idea of perfectionism? In what ways has this mindset crept into your own thought processes?
- Why do you think you try to hide your imperfections? With whom can you be open about your imperfections?
- Do you tend to view others as more perfect than they are? Why or why not? Do you view yourself similarly?
- What can you do to make a conscious habit of being honest about your struggles with God? What about being honest with yourself?
- What are some things you have learned about yourself and your relationship with God through this story? How can you use this information to help you grow in your faith?

SO MUCH TO DO, SO LITTLE TIME

I keep myself pretty busy. In fact, I keep myself so busy that I often am told I run myself into the ground. I enjoy being busy, but sometimes it can get to be too much. After a chaotic schedule like the one I tend to keep, a nice relaxing evening can sound like a myth. When summer hits, like most people, I am beyond thrilled. However, as my friends go off and celebrate, stay up late, and hang out, I spend the first part of my summer sleeping. It sounds very boring, I know, but it is necessary for me to recuperate. I take as much me-time as I can, enjoying the peace and quiet I have missed for so long. However, after a week or so of this, it gets old. I become restless with boredom and overcompensate by filling my schedule once again. Suddenly, the schedule that was so baren only moments before is now overflowing with practices, lessons, or volunteer hours. The next thing I know, the end of summer has arrived and I have forgotten to rest once again.

It is surprising how difficult resting truly is. There are so many things that we want to do! A thousand things vie for our attention at once. Time spent not being productive feels like time being wasted, despite how untrue that is. It is so easy to forget to rest. I often find myself giving in to the gravitational pull of self-assigned work. I'm sure many of you have found yourself in the same boat.

It took a long time for me to realize what the culprit of my busyness was. The problem was *me* and my selfish desires. I had shifted my priorities from His plans for me to my plans for myself. I had too many things that *I* wanted to do. Just because something is a good activity doesn't mean that you're supposed to be doing it. I couldn't say no, and I ended up overwhelmed and stressed. They were good things, but they weren't good for *me*. I concluded that I should be bringing every decision before God, not just the big ones. He knows what is best for me, so why wouldn't I ask Him? As I continued to do this, I was surprised to find that He was leading me away from certain activities. I loved them, but I also saw how much they were taking out of me. God knew they weren't good for me even if I couldn't see it myself.

Not surprisingly, this practice began to clear up a lot of my time. I found I had been giving *a lot* of my time to activities that were not beneficial or rewarding for me to be a part of. In this free time I had created, I was able to spend more alone time with God. I talked to Him more, studied the Bible more, and learned more about myself. That's why we lean on God. He knows what is best for us. He knows what we should or should not pursue. There was a noticeable difference in my stress and anxiety as I continued to listen to His guidance. My exhaustion was replaced with His peace. It is crazy how spending a little bit of time with God can change absolutely everything.

Take time to talk to God about your commitments. Sincerely ask Him for guidance about your decisions. Sit in silence, still in His presence. That is one of the most healing, powerful, and important things you can do. That is when he speaks to you. Remember that He wants you to enjoy life! However, He knows you can only truly handle so much. Let Him guide you to those decisions. Enjoy the activities, but don't forget to enjoy the peace as well.

> *Peace I leave with you; my peace I give you. I do not give to you as the world gives. Do not let your hearts be troubled and do not be afraid.*
> —John 14:27 (ESV)

PERSONAL REFLECTION QUESTIONS

> What is a story from your life that is similar to the story shared above? How did it make you feel? How did you react to it?

> Evaluate your schedule. Are there any activities that you know you should be doing that you are putting off for your own agenda? What are those personal activities? Most likely that is God trying to tell you how to clean up your messy life's schedule.

> Do the people that influence you have their priorities in check? Do they take the time to keep God in their schedule? If so, what can you do to reflect their positive habits? If not, how can you avoid letting their bad habits affect you?

> What are things you turn to for peace that aren't God? Do you have a healthy relationship with these things?

> What brings you peace? Why? How can you use this to connect with God more closely?

> What are some things you have learned about yourself and your relationship with God through this story? How can you use this information to help you grow in your faith?

CAN'T MESS THIS UP

With how focused the world is on finding "true love," it can become easy to focus on finding "the one." It's an easy thing to obsess about. Isn't it beautiful to think that somewhere out there, God made someone who is perfect for you? They are strong in their faith, attractive … and nowhere to be found. Talk about frustrating! This mindset quickly changes our emotions, motives, and experiences. When we finally meet someone that we think could be it, we begin to overthink every little detail. We find ourselves overwhelmed by trying to design a perfect relationship. I can remember many restless nights, my mind brimming with questions. *Are we still friends? Are we as close as we used to be? Did I do something to offend them? Do they even like me anymore? I can't mess this up!* These thoughts plague our minds and souls with anxiety. They ruin our days, our nights, and every moment in between. Many of us so strongly desire to have a perfect relationship that we believe we must change ourselves to fit what we believe other people's qualifications are.

Relationships are, in fact, wonderful. I probably don't need to convince you of that. All it takes is one glance at a social media network, a pop song, or a movie to tell us that. Romantic relationships are one of the most commercialized relationships in the world (if not the most). To make matters worse, those in the so-called perfect relationships almost always appear perfect, themselves. They have the perfect body, voice, talent, laugh, you name it! The expectations we have created through watching and hearing about fake relationships are unattainable and toxic. In reality, no one is that perfect—and certainly no relationship is as perfect as it appears on screen.

The love that God wants us to pursue doesn't include all the falseness that you see online. If you are approaching a love that God is in support and center of, you shouldn't be worrying about changing who you are to fit the expectations of the world. True love won't care about those things. They will love you because of who you are in Christ. A real love is not built on fleeting attributes, like beauty, talent, or fame. It is built on the love of God. That is the only foundation that will stand the test of time. He is the only foundation that will never crack.

Reaching the world's version of perfection is not going to find you true love. Believing that lie will only lead you down a long path of disappointment and sadness. If you are supposed to be in a relationship, you must let God be the one to orchestrate it. If you're following God first, then His perfect plan will follow. Trust in holy wisdom. He wants what is best for you. Release your life into His hands, listen to His calling, and follow when He directs you. That is the only way you will create a life that will bring you true happiness. If it is all in God's hands, then you can't mess this up. Rest in that peace. Seek Him and He will guide you towards where you are meant to be.

You will seek me and find me, when you seek me with all your heart.
—Jeremiah 29:13 (ESV)

And those who know your name put their trust in you, for you, O Lord, have not forsaken those who seek you.
—Psalms 9:10 (ESV)

The Lord is good to those who wait for him, to the soul who seeks him.
—Lamentations 3:25 (ESV)

PERSONAL REFLECTION QUESTIONS

> What is a story from your life that is similar to the story shared above? How did it make you feel? How did you react to it?

> What are some beliefs about relationships (platonic or romantic) that you have adopted due to culture?

> Are there any relationships in your life that might not have the right motive at heart? Why do you think this?

> Are your relationships pushing you closer to God, or closer to the world's ideas of love and acceptance? What can you do to change that if needed?

> Just because a friend isn't Christian doesn't mean we shouldn't be close to him or her. However, we must be careful that our non-Christian friends do not influence our belief system in negative ways. What are some safeguards you can establish

for yourself that will allow you to minister to them without having their negative beliefs affect you?

➤ What are some things you have learned about yourself and your relationship with God through this story? How can you use this information to help you grow in your faith?

COULDN'T YOU HEAR?

In high school, my drama team went on a small tour. That tour holds some of my favorite memories to this day. However, it was often a challenge for me to figure out where I was supposed to be going. Because we were performing at multiple different schools every single day, it was easy to become directionally confused. It didn't help that I am naturally awful with directions. I'm fairly confident that I got lost at least twice in every school we visited. There was one school we visited that my brain simply could not wrap around. I had learned from my mistakes in the past and took a friend with me this time. However, that didn't seem to prove useful as we found ourselves lost and alone in the middle of an empty hallway, the bus scheduled to leave in approximately five minutes. Right as we were about to panic, a student rounded the corner. Thank goodness!

We ran over to ask him directions but ended up with a very funny interaction instead. "Hey! We're from the school that just put on that play for you guys. We're totally lost, and our bus is leaving in five minutes; do you know which way the exit is?"

I was expecting a brief explanation.

Nope.

We were both surprised when, instead of pointing us the right way, he sighed deeply. "It's *shaped* like an *H*. For *hills*. Like the name, obviously." He stared at us, seemingly incredulous as to why we wouldn't know that already.

I stuttered for a second, searching for a way to respond. "I … we … um. Thanks." I spun around faster than a top, yanked my friend's arm, and bolted away from the awkward conversation.

Once we were out of his sight, we doubled over laughing at both ourselves and the conversation. It was just so uncomfortably *awkward*. That experience quickly became an ongoing joke between the two of us.

About six months later, both of my school's varsity basketball teams made it to the state championship. It was a very exciting day, and my teammates and I were thrilled. My friend decided to come to support my team, and we stayed afterward to cheer for the guys. The game was normal until halftime hit. Then, it got weird. Suddenly, some random guy from the other team's crowd jumped up, ran out *on the court*, and began trying to get the entire gymnasium to do the wave with him! We couldn't believe it!

We were all laughing, confused at the strange sight in front of us. Then, my friend shot out of her chair and began excitedly shouting, "It's the H guy! It's the H guy! No way! Look!" I couldn't see him very well from the stands, but listening to his voice, I could tell immediately it was him.

I turned to my friend, surprised and impressed with her memory. "How could you tell that was him?" I asked.

"Couldn't you hear his voice?" she said. "It was obviously him."

Speech has more power than you would expect. It has vast potential to do both good and evil. Unfortunately, instead of using our speech to encourage others, people have begun to take pride in how vilely they can speak. Vulgar language has flooded music, radio, television, and even common speech. It has become normal to hear degrading insults and repulsive language on a daily basis.

Thankfully, this is not everyone. There are people out there fighting this negative narrative. It takes quite a bit of self-control to keep from being influenced by this behavior. It is not easy, as I am sure you know. While motivational speakers and teachers are seeking to preach this message, they can only do so much. Real change is going to come when we decide to take a stand for our beliefs. It takes only one person to start a chain reaction.

Unfortunately, rather than a chain reaction of people making better choices, it seems a negative chain reaction has occurred. It saddens me when I hear many fellow Christians using filthy language, unashamedly. We cannot expect those without Christ to have Christian convictions. However, there is a disappointing amount of us who simply cast these convictions aside. It seems we have simply given up. We have decided that it doesn't matter if we hear or even say these words. This is a large issue that is often not addressed as often as it should be. We have accepted the negativity in media, toxic ideals, and inappropriate language as a way of life. We don't fight it anymore. We have stopped caring how we represent ourselves through our speech.

Just like my friend and I knew the H guy from his voice, others will know you by your speech. Are your words kind and encouraging, or uninterested, rude, and dismissive? Our speech should be foreign to the world because we follow rules the world doesn't understand. We should not fit in the crowd of the world, especially when it comes to our speech. Luckily, we've been given an example. Jesus was well known for the kindness He showed to those who were unkind to Him. Consider the trial before His crucifixion in Luke 23 followed by His prayer and pleading to God for their forgiveness. He didn't fit the narrative of the world, but rather stood out as an example of love, mercy, and kindness. As His followers, we are called to do the same.

Let the words you say and the way you say them lead others to the love of Christ. You are known by your speech—let your speech lead them to Christ. Follow the higher calling we have been given. You never know who may recognize you or see the one you serve through your speech.

Let your conversation be always full of grace, seasoned with salt, so that you may know how to answer everyone.
—Colossians 4:6 (ESV)

Do not let any unwholesome talk come out of your mouths, but only what is helpful for building others up according to their needs, that it may benefit those who listen.
—Ephesians 4:29 (ESV)

She speaks with wisdom, and faithful instruction is on her tongue.
—Proverbs 31:26 (ESV)

PERSONAL REFLECTION QUESTIONS

- What is a story from your life that is similar to the story shared above? How did it make you feel? How did you react to it?
- Ask a few people to describe your speaking style in three descriptive words. Ask for their honest opinion. The best way to know how people perceive you is to ask them. Use what they tell you as your basis. How can you change people's perception of your speech to make those descriptive words more closely resemble God's?
- The words we listen to are just as important as the words we say. Evaluate the things you choose to listen to, whether it be music, the speech choices of your friends, podcasts, etc. Are these words edifying and positive, or are they full of vulgar

language and inappropriate content? What steps can you take to change that?

- How often do you think about how people perceive your speech? Many people pay attention to clothing, posture, or hobbies, but speech is often taken for granted. Take the day to pay close attention to people's speech. Record your findings and reflect on them.

- Are you using your speech not only to let others know you are a Christian but to reach others through love? It is important that we use our speech not only to help ourselves spiritually but also to reach others. Think of someone who could use encouragement today and reach out to that person! Use your speech for the good of others, too.

- What are some things you have learned about yourself and your relationship with God through this story? How can you use this information to help you grow in your faith?

MY PLAYLIST

I don't know about you, but music is a huge part of my life. No matter what time of day it is, it seems a song is always stuck in my head. Since I tend to internalize my music, what I listen to has a major effect on my mood. This has the potential to be extremely beneficial. For instance, if I am sad, I turn on happier music and I'm generally good to go (at least for a little bit). However, it can also cause issues. I internalize *all* my music, including sad songs. I find that sad songs are often lyrically gorgeous, and as I am quite fond of writing, that is important to me. Therefore, I have a natural love of sad music (I promise that sentence is not actually as depressing as it sounds). However, this can cause me to head into a negative emotional spiral. If I wasn't already upset about something, I have now unintentionally convinced myself to be sad. It is a highly unfortunate side effect. That negative spiral can be difficult to come back from, which I didn't realize for a long time. I had no idea how negatively my music choices had been affecting me until one day I reviewed my playlist and found almost *exclusively* sad music. It's nice to appreciate lyrics, but my playlist had gotten out of hand. I had to do something about it quickly.

I soon began to add worship, praise, and fun music to my playlist. It was surprising how quickly my mood changed. I had never understood just how accurate the phrase "junk in, junk out" was until that moment. That was a mistake I intend to never let happen again.

As Christians, we must be aware of what messages we are feeding ourselves. What we put into our minds will come out in our emotions and actions. That's a big responsibility. Be mindful to introduce yourself to ideas and messages that draw you closer to God. It isn't wrong to listen to a sad song. You were made to have emotions. By all means, feel them! But make sure to keep them in check. We are told multiple times in Scripture that we will take on the traits of the things we surround ourselves with. Like Philippians 4:8 says, "Finally, brothers and sisters, whatever is true, whatever is noble, whatever is right, whatever is pure, whatever is lovely, whatever is admirable—if anything is excellent or praiseworthy—think about such things." This idea comes into effect in every area of our lives. We hear many different messages throughout the day, which means what you choose to listen to is extremely important. What you hear alters how you think, which ultimately alters how you behave. In a world filled with negative messages, it is of utmost importance that what we choose to listen to is edifying and pure. We must combat the messages being forced upon us. We cannot give in to the lies being broadcast throughout our culture. We must find ways to include His truth in our daily lives.

Knowing and hearing His truths repeatedly is the only way we are going to be able to fight the lies around us. Instead of submerging ourselves in the negative narratives of the world, let us fill our minds with the love and hope of God. Let His joy and peace take over your soul, filling you with love and happiness. That is a *much* better way to spend your day.

Do not conform to the pattern of this world, but be transformed by the renewing of your mind. Then you will be able to test and approve what God's will is—his good, pleasing and perfect will.
—Romans 12:2 (ESV)

Finally, brothers and sisters, whatever is true, whatever is noble, whatever is right, whatever is pure, whatever is lovely, whatever is admirable—if anything is excellent or praiseworthy—think about such things.
—Philippians 4:8 (ESV)

PERSONAL REFLECTION QUESTIONS

➤ What is a story from your life that is similar to the story shared above? How did it make you feel? How did you react to it?

➤ What are you surrounding yourself with that could affect your emotions? Are the books you read pure and wholesome? What about the content in the movies you watch, or the language involved with them? Take a minute and think about the things that surround you. Could they possibly be affecting what you think or how you feel? Are they separating you from spending time with God?

➤ When you are going through a hard time, what do you naturally turn to? Why do you think this is? What could you do to make it more centered around God?

➤ Look at your playlists, movies, and book series. What messages are they sending? Are they overall positive and uplifting? Do they resemble the traits of a Christian? Or are they falling prey to poor habits? What actions can you take to rectify that?

- It is easy to trust God in the good times but much harder when things aren't going well. What are some verses or song lyrics that remind you of God's goodness and love? Write them down! Read them the next time you are struggling.

- What are some things you have learned about yourself and your relationship with God through this story? How can you use this information to help you grow in your faith?

OUT OF NOWHERE

The bell that dismissed us from school rang out loud and clear. I bolted toward the door, quickly grabbing my change of clothes for drama rehearsal. I headed over to rehearsal, excited to get to work on one of my favorite hobbies after such a long day of school. As I entered the room, I made eye contact with a friend, smiling as I remembered a funny story I had to tell her.

I walked over to her, laughing. "Hey, you know what's the absolute worst?" I asked, about to let her in on my comical experience.

The words had barely left my lips when another girl entered the room, slowly looked me up and down, and sighed. With a hand resting on her cocked hip, she promptly answered the question not intended for her. "What's the worst? Oh, I know. How about when someone thinks everything is *all about her* when in reality, no one cares what she does at all?"

She spat her words out, turned around, and left me to my whirlwind of thoughts. Clearly, her comments were directed toward me, but I couldn't figure out why. *Did I do something to offend her? Was I really being too self-centered, and just didn't realize it? What if other people thought that about me too?* Tears pricked my eyes as buried doubts and fears resurfaced. Quietly, I packed up my clothes, stuffed them in my locker, and shuffled to rehearsal. Her attack had come out of nowhere, and I was left unprepared and hurt.

It seems like bad things always come unexpectedly and last forever, but good things tend to take tons of work and disappear very quickly. It is a frustrating dichotomy. Why can't we get a nice, clear warning when things are about to go poorly? Some giant, flashing lights would be nice. That way we could at least mentally prepare ourselves for it. But, as I am sure you know, we don't get loud announcements or flashing lights to warn us. Instead, we get a rather unfortunate surprise.

I don't know about you, but I don't always respond the best to surprises. I prefer to have a planned, detailed map of what I can expect in my day. When a large event throws off my rhythm, it can be hard for me to recover. I begin to stress about my workload, time management, emotional stability, my family's reactions—you name it! My mind is overtaken with planning for anything that could go wrong. I unintentionally hand over control of my thoughts, actions, and emotions to the situation in front of me.

Do you ever struggle with this? It is difficult when something catches you off guard. Without even realizing it, it consumes your thoughts, sucks the joy out of your days, and steals the sleep from your nights. This is why Satan uses surprise to attack us. He knows it is the best way to catch us unprepared. He often catches us at the perfect time, fooling us into falling prey to worry. However, we tend to forget that we have someone on our side who is never caught off guard, never unprepared, and always ready to fight our battles with us.

God reminds us repeatedly in scripture that He is here for us. He wants us to remember that He holds absolute power, truth, and knowledge. Sure, Satan may have landed you a good kick in the gut. But that doesn't mean that the battle is over. Stand back up and remind yourself who is fighting by your side. We will always fail when we place the responsibility of success on ourselves. However, when we hand it over to God, we have made our first step toward success. He is fighting (and winning) every single battle. He is never unprepared.

Great is our Lord, and abundant in power; his understanding is beyond measure.
—Psalm 146:5 (ESV)

Even before a word is on my tongue, behold, O Lord, you know it altogether.
—Psalm 139:4 (ESV)

For whenever our heart condemns us, God is greater than our heart, and he knows everything.
—1 John 3:20 (ESV)

PERSONAL REFLECTION QUESTIONS

➤ What is a story from your life that is similar to the story shared above? How did it make you feel? How did you react to it?

➤ Is there an event that has recently occurred in your life that caught you off guard? How did you respond to it? What changes could you make to begin to respond better?

➤ Do you struggle with giving negative events power over your thoughts or actions? What could you do to intentionally redirect yourself?

- Is it difficult for you to trust that God already has figured out how to manage this conflict? Why? What are you putting your faith in instead?
- Describe a time in your life when you saw God moving when you didn't expect it. Did this event help you to believe that He has everything under control? Why or why not?
- What are some things you have learned about yourself and your relationship with God through this story? How can you use this information to help you grow in your faith?

CALLED TO LOVE

While meeting new people can be exciting, it can also cause a lot of uncertainty. I was feeling all the excitement *and* anxiety when I began freshman orientation at college. I was in a new place, with new responsibilities, surrounded by completely new people. It was overwhelming trying to match faces with names, majors, and personalities. I tried to keep a mental list of the people I thought I might get along with but only ended up confusing myself more in the process. I knew everyone was in the same boat as me, yet I felt completely alone. Truthfully, we all just needed a friend.

As the week continued, I slowly but surely began to make connections with people. We got to know each other more by telling stories, talking about our passions, and going to events together. Our personalities began to shine through the façades we had put up when we first met. It was strange to see people slowly take down their social walls and reveal their true personalities. I realized that my original perceptions about some of the people had changed ... then I panicked. What if the things they found out about me changed their opinion of me? I began to worry. *I don't have many friends on campus, and I can't afford to lose any. I really like these people, but what if I end up the odd one out again?* Eventually, I was so consumed by these thoughts that I stopped sharing things about myself. If I didn't change anything about myself, they wouldn't change their opinion of me. I became a fly on a wall. I was seen but never heard from. That way I would be safe.

About a month into the semester, I was returning to my dorm for the night when I saw my roommate had invited a guest over. I didn't mind, but I also didn't feel like socializing. So, I climbed up on my bed, put in my earbuds, and began my homework. However, right before I turned on my music, I heard them talking about the "calling of a Christian." I was intrigued and decided to silently listen to their conversation.

The guest paused for a moment, then said, "The call of a Christian is not *to be loved* but *to love.*" This sentence, as simple and plain as it was, stopped me in my tracks. I immediately reached over for a pen and paper to write it down. It was such a simple concept in theory but so profound in meaning.

I am sure I'd heard this concept explained before, but this time it hit differently. This time, instead of simply understanding the message, I felt it personally. It applied. I realized I'd been so concerned about *being loved* that I had forgotten *to* love.

In this world, it should not be our goal to be loved. It is not our objective to have large friend groups, famous reputations, or high social status. It is, however, our job to throw away those desires in pursuit of the truths of Christ. They are wonderful things to have, yes. However, they must never become our focus. We are often tricked into believing that to love others, they must love us back. While that is always beautiful, sometimes it doesn't work like that. Sometimes we are called to be selfless and sacrifice for people who wouldn't do that for us. This will lead others to see Christ in you. It sets you apart from the world, causing you to shine with His love. By loving others instead of focusing on being loved, you may just be the one that points them back to Him. We are called to love. Christ will take care of the rest.

A new command I give you: Love one another. As I have loved you, so you must love one another. By this everyone will know that you are my disciples, if you love one another.
—John 13:34–35 (ESV)

Then make my joy complete by being like-minded, having the same love, being one in spirit and of one mind.
—Philippians 2:2 (ESV)

Dear friends, let us love one another, for love comes from God. Everyone who loves has been born of God and knows God.
—1 John 4:7 (ESV)

PERSONAL REFLECTION QUESTIONS

> What is a story from your life that is similar to the story shared above? How did it make you feel? How did you react to it?

> Though we are sometimes called into difficult relationships, it is important to also establish healthy ones. Who in your life do you believe both gives and receives love well? Do you do the same for them?

> In what areas in your life do you need to focus on giving more love?

> Think about the people in your life that pour into you. In what ways could you thank them?

> Examine your relationship with social media. How much time are you spending feeding into the world's version of popularity and love? What steps can you take to avoid doing this?

- What are some things you have learned about yourself and your relationship with God through this story? How can you use this information to help you grow in your faith?

I WILL

In life, we tend to expect more from ourselves than anyone else. We refuse to excuse our mistakes, blaming them on our many inadequacies. Where we would give others encouragement and grace, we give ourselves constant and unrelenting criticism. We congratulate others on the smallest achievements, elated for their success. But when it comes to *our* little victories, we brush them off as if they were completely insignificant. It's as if we tell ourselves that if we are not the best, we are worthless. I often find myself in an "I will" mindset, telling myself there is no option but absolute success. I put an unrealistic amount of pressure on myself to always succeed. However, this pressure is often what causes us to stumble in the first place. It causes our plans to backfire, damaging the situation we were trying to perfect.

It is natural to desire to do your best and to work hard to achieve success. However, such a mindset can be easily manipulated. Just because you want to do something to the best of your ability does not necessarily mean that it will be better than everyone else. We have all been called to different talents, professions, and passions. We can always do our best. We can't always *be* the best. That's okay. Don't put pressure on yourself that isn't there.

It can be difficult to adopt the right mindset after battling such a toxic one. This is especially true if it has leaked into your spiritual life. So many people believe that if they are not flawless, God wants nothing to do with them. They keep a mental list of every single mistake they've ever made, knowing that each entry means separation from perfection. All they can see when they look in the mirror is a big sign that says "FAILURE". They believe that because they aren't the best, they are nothing at all. This is not how God looks at us.

God knows that we have all failed. That is why He sent His Son to die on the cross for our sins. It is through His sacrifice that we have been made pure. None of us have what it takes to reach perfection. It doesn't matter how hard we try; it is impossible. We are fallen, fallible, and prone to sin. It is not in our power to remove sin from our lives. However, that doesn't mean it cannot be removed.

Once we have been made aware of our problem, there is little we can do but bring it to God. It is not in your power to save yourself. That is something that only God can do. It is often hard to view our lives without us in charge of it. We prefer to grip our problems tightly and refuse to relinquish control until the situation has been solved. However, it is only God that can solve our problems. We must release if we desire remedy.

Our stubbornness and willpower get us no closer to our desired outcome. A tight grip on control means a loose faithfulness in God's power. Remember, it is through release that we gain a comprehensive hold on reality. It is our faith in Him that guides us toward our true end.

In their hearts humans plan their course, but the Lord establishes their steps.
—Proverbs 16:9 (ESV)

In all your ways acknowledge him, and he will make straight your paths.
—Proverbs 3:6 (ESV)

I know, O Lord, that the way of man is not in himself, that it is not in man who walks to direct his steps.
—Jeremiah 10:23 (ESV)

Your word is a lamp to my feet and a light to my path.
—Psalm 119:105 (ESV)

PERSONAL REFLECTION QUESTIONS

> What is a story from your life that is similar to the story shared above? How did it make you feel? How did you react to it?

> What activities are you trying to control in your life right now? Has it worked so far? Why or why not?

> Think about some times in the past when you tried to control change. Was it difficult? Did it seem never to progress the way you thought it should have? Do you believe it would have gone differently had you let God take the reins?

> Why do you personally feel the need for control? Take a second to think about why you work the way you do. That can be important in leading to self-discovery.

> Think about the things in life that are causing you pressure right now. Why do you think you feel so afflicted by them?

What can you do to start shifting the pressure off of you individually and giving it to God?

> What are some things you have learned about yourself and your relationship with God through this story? How can you use this information to help you grow in your faith?

MAXIMIZE YOUR "MUNDANE"

It can be very easy to get lost in the trap of comparing our lives to others. As someone who has had to miss out on quite a few opportunities, this has been a mental battle I have faced for years. I no doubt have been very blessed in my life, but it is so much easier to focus on what you've lost than what you've gained. It felt like I was continually missing out on experiences that everybody else got to have. Comparing your life to someone else's is a dangerous and lonely path. I had fallen in, and I couldn't quite seem to climb my way out.

When we feel this way, we often look for others who might relate to us. Due to the nature of our culture, the first place we usually turn to is social media. Unfortunately, that is about the farthest thing from helpful. Social media is full of people's best representations of themselves. Every post is full of friends getting together (without you), amazing vacations (that you never get to go on), parties (that you weren't invited to), and so on. It is draining and exhausting. Instead of making us feel heard or understood, we are told the lie that everyone is doing better than us. Rather than feeling reassured or encouraged, we continue to add more to our pile of misery as we scroll photo after photo of things that we don't have. We forget how easy it is to play a part online. Real life is so much harder than it looks on screen.

I had been thoroughly convinced everyone was living a far better life than I was. I mean, everyone else was going to parties, taking vacations, and making new friends. What was I doing? Sitting on my unmade bed, with a pile of laundry on my desk, doing chemistry homework. Not the most exciting experience in the world.

One day as I was scrolling social media, I saw a particularly frustrating post. There was a beautiful girl, with her beautiful boyfriend, laughing with tons of other beautiful friends, all on a yacht in the tropical islands, celebrating a huge milestone in her musical career. Not to mention the thousands of likes and comments below the post itself. This girl had everything you could ever want! I was happy for her and excited about her success. However, I couldn't help but feel inferior once again. I didn't have a single one of the things she did. As I continued to scroll, it only added to my pity party. Everyone was beautiful, successful, and *oh-so-happy*. Sure, I'm a happy person, but I have my bad days. This was clearly one of them. Seeing their smiling faces was like salt in a wound that afternoon.

I had finally had enough. I turned to my friend about my irritation, wondering if she battled this feeling as well. Surely, she was experiencing the same frustrations. She didn't get to go to fancy parties or amazing vacations, either. However, our conversation did not go the way I expected. Her response was something I don't believe I will ever forget. She said, "It does stink that we have to go through this. It is ridiculous. But if I think of my favorite times in life … well, the most fun I have ever had was in the mundane."

I stood there silent for a moment as I thought about what she had said and the truth behind it. I was focused on the grandiose opportunities I was missing, and though they are fun and filled with amazing memories, she was right. Real relationships are built in your everyday life, with everyday people, through everyday situations. I had been missing the point the whole time.

Our relationship with God works the same way. We do not build trust, faith, or love through the grand moments in our journey. We do this through everyday scenarios. That's not to say the larger events in your spiritual walk aren't important. Moments such as answered prayer or long-awaited success are amazing, and you should enjoy them. However, the status of your relationship with God should not be built on these emotional highs. There is so much more to your relationship with Him.

Don't let everyday things go to waste. God does not only walk with us when we are doing something that seems significant. He walks with us everywhere, all the time. He is present in our mundane. He wants you to include Him while you're drinking a cup of coffee. He wants to talk to you while you're waiting in line at the grocery store. He desires to spend time with you when you're daydreaming or bored with homework. It might not be something big or revolutionary. That doesn't mean it isn't something important. We must learn how to take our mundane and maximize its potential. It is here that Christ meets you daily. It is here that we grow.

Come near to God and he will come near to you.
—James 4:8 (ESV)

Be diligent in these matters; give yourself wholly to them, so that everyone may see your progress.
—1 Timothy 4:15 (ESV)

But grow in the grace and knowledge of our Lord and Savior Jesus Christ. To him be glory both now and forever! Amen.
—2 Peter 3:18 (ESV)

PERSONAL REFLECTION QUESTIONS

- What is a story from your life that is similar to the story shared above? How did it make you feel? How did you react to it?

- Both the big and little events in our Spiritual lives are important. Reflect on a time you went through spiritual growth in both scenarios. How have you used these to continue growing after the events?

- What activities are you doing in your mundane periods of life that will keep you focused on God? How are you connecting with Him daily?

- Are you paying attention in your daily life to ways God might be trying to talk to you? Or, are you so focused on a one-way conversation that you've missed Him talking?

- What is something you've learned about your relationship with God or the nature of God while in the "mundane" this week?

- What are some things you have learned about yourself and your relationship with God through this story? How can you use this information to help you grow in your faith?

PUZZLING PERSPECTIVES

Isn't it amazing when you make a spiritual connection with someone? In my opinion, it is one of the greatest joys in life. It is incredible to think that God has placed specific people in our path for us to interact with, learn from, and grow beside. Sometimes, you meet this person and you connect right away. Other times, it requires a bit of work to figure out if you're a match or not. I have been left consistently baffled as to whom God chooses for me to connect with. They are almost never the people I expect. Instead, they are usually people whom I thought I had no chance of connecting with. Though this happens quite often in my life, I am somehow always surprised by it. I never see it coming.

This experience occurred again recently. And, again, I was quite surprised. I was *especially* surprised because I had never had an exceptional relationship with this person. In fact, there were times we couldn't stand each other. Our relationship had been on the mend for a while, but at this point, we had simply reached mutual indifference. Neither of us wanted to continue the negativity, but we also didn't care to pursue a friendship. We decided it was safer to keep it neutral.

I had almost completely forgotten about that relationship by the time New Year's arrived. That holiday always made me laugh.

While Christmas was known for love and peace, Thanksgiving for fellowship, and Easter for hope, New Year's was infamous for unfulfilled promises. Not the best reputation to have. I had decided that this year I was going to beat the system. I was actually going to keep my New Year's resolution!

Instead of giving myself something easy, like not eating as many sweets, I made the ambitious choice to focus on mending relationships. Unfortunately, that meant I had to engage in a lot of conversations I had been avoiding. Sure, I wanted my relationships fixed, but I didn't want to have to be the one to fix them. It's painful and scary. In hindsight, if I wanted an easy New Year's resolution, I really should have chosen anything *but* this. But a promise is a promise, so I pushed through.

A few weeks later, I observed this individual in a situation that showed them in a completely new perspective. It was as if through seeing this one event, all the puzzle pieces were put together. I could finally see the whole picture. Everything that had happened between us made sense. Suddenly, instead of the emotional numbness I had developed toward them, I felt compassion and love. I felt myself being called to break the barrier between us and pursue a friendship. I was certainly wary and a bit skeptical at first. But as time went on, it was clear that furthering this relationship had been God's desire.

As we began to get to know each other on a more personal level, we found that we had shared many similar circumstances in life. It was as if God has perfectly connected our life experiences so that we could grow in faith together. He knew that we needed each other, even if we couldn't see that for ourselves. That realization was one of the most beautiful moments I had ever experienced. I still think about the evolution of our friendship quite often. It wasn't what either of us expected, but we are both eternally grateful that it happened.

God often works in ways we don't expect. Sometimes, through people that we don't expect. When God draws us to someone, know that He has a reason for it. It may take you a long time to figure out why you have been called to a specific person. Sometimes the answer remains unclear. However, there is always a purpose. He wants to do a beautiful work both in and through you. When His plans are revealed, you will stand in awe of the amazing things He has done. Our fallen perspectives can be puzzling, but His are always clear.

Bear with each other and forgive one another if any of you has a grievance against someone. Forgive as the Lord forgave you.
—Colossians 3:13 (ESV)

Iron sharpens iron, and one man sharpens another.
—Proverbs 27:17 (ESV)

Whoever covers an offense seeks love, but he who repeats a matter separates close friends.
—Proverbs 17:9 (ESV)

A new commandment I give to you, that you love one another: just as I have loved you, you also are to love one another.
—John 13:34 (ESV)

PERSONAL REFLECTION QUESTIONS

▸ What is a story from your life that is similar to the story shared above? How did it make you feel? How did you react to it?

▸ Do you have a relationship that has been damaged over time? Has the stress of life pulled the two of you apart? Do you feel the need to restore that relationship? Why or why not?

▸ Why do you believe that relationship was damaged in the first place? Have you been viewing the situation with your perspective on your hurt, or with your perspective on God's love?

▸ Many relationships will take time to heal. Things will not suddenly get better the moment you reach out. What are some things you can do to continue to try to heal these relationships and keep your perspective in the right place?

▸ Take a moment to pray for anyone that you know might be struggling right now. Is there anyone on your heart? Try reaching out to them this week and lending them some encouragement.

▸ What are some things you have learned about yourself and your relationship with God through this story? How can you use this information to help you grow in your faith?

FEARLESS

Lately, I have been seeing ads all over the place talking about being "fearless." They tell us to be fearless in our pursuit of happiness, be fearless in our endeavors for the future, be fearless in what we believe—the list goes on and on. Though these are seemingly positive messages, there is a concerning underlying theme connecting them. This theme has been running rampant in our culture. Many don't even realize the magnitude of its effects on our perception of reality. The theme? It is all about being fearless for *your own gain*.

It is not being fearless that is the issue. Christ calls us to be fearless many times. However, our fearlessness comes from the knowledge of His power, love, and might. It comes from an internal understanding of His innate goodness and eternal plan. The fearlessness that is being advertised to us has nothing to do with that. Their fearlessness comes from a selfish desire for fame, fortune, or beauty. It stems not from goodness, but from acting as our own god. They tell us that we can have whatever we want if we aren't scared. They tell us that we can make any fleeting desire become our reality. They want us to believe that our happiness should be our top priority. Scripture clearly states that this is not true. While God loves us and wants us to be happy, He knows what will bring us *true* happiness and peace. Usually, it doesn't come from what we believe it will. The world, however, tells us to unashamedly go after every whim and will that we please. That will never bring us the happiness we desire. Our pursuit of fearlessness should not be for personal gain but for the furthering of His kingdom and His will for our lives. That is where we find true joy.

Unfortunately, "fearless" is one of the last labels I hear given to modern Christianity. In the past, Christianity used to be celebrated and praised. It was a normal thing to be able to talk about your beliefs in public and not be faced with mass opposition. Our world today tells an entirely different story. We are now attacked with negative labels and assumptions at every turn. We are told we are "intolerable of other religions," "too stuck up to know what is right," or even that we "hate people different from us." It seems no matter how hard we try, we simply cannot break this negative perception. Though it is the farthest thing from the truth, this is the world's perception of us. Instead of fighting against this narrative, we have shied away and hidden, living our convictions silently. We have become a fearful generation.

We cannot continue to conform to the world's demand for our silence. No good comes from hiding in the shadows. We are called to be light. Darkness cannot be where light resides. We must step out into the world with the confidence of Christ. Our mouths have been sealed for too long.

It is time that we learn to be fearless in our pursuit of spiritual awakening. We were made to stand out and stand up for what we believe. Just because you are the only one in the room standing for what is right does not mean you are standing alone. Your brothers and sisters in faith are cheering you on and fighting the battle with you. Have confidence, knowing that the King of all Creation is on your side. You are fighting a battle that is already won. He is walking with you every step of the way. Your light shines brightest in the darkest of places. Go forth fearlessly.

Finally, be strong in the Lord and in his mighty power. Put on the full armor of God, so that you can take your stand against the devil's schemes. For our struggle is not against flesh and blood, but against the rulers, against the authorities, against the powers of this dark world and against the spiritual forces of evil in the heavenly realms. Therefore, put on the full armor of God, so that when the day of evil comes, you may be able to stand your ground, and after you have done everything, to stand. Stand firm then, with the belt of truth buckled around your waist, with the breastplate of righteousness in place, and with your feet fitted with the readiness that comes from the gospel of peace. In addition to all this, take up the shield of faith, with which you can extinguish all the flaming arrows of the evil one. Take the helmet of salvation and the sword of the Spirit, which is the word of God.
—Ephesians 6:10–17 (ESV)

PERSONAL REFLECTION QUESTIONS

> What is a story from your life that is similar to the story shared above? How did it make you feel? How did you react to it?

> What are some things you are fearless in your pursuit of? What are some areas you struggle with?

> What are some triggers or situations that cause you to fear being bold in your faith? Why is this? What can you do to combat this?

- What are some examples from your own life when you were bold about your faith? What happened? What about some moments you were timid? What happened? Looking back, what would you change?
- What can you do to encourage others to be fearless in their faith? Who can you reach out to that will help you in the same way?
- What are some things you have learned about yourself and your relationship with God through this story? How can you use this information to help you grow in your faith?

BIG KIDS

Do you remember walking into church when you were little and seeing your absolute favorite "big kid"? That always meant it was going to be a good day at church. Seeing them was often the highlight of my morning! They were the epitome of what we wanted to become as children. Everything they did, we wanted to copy. I was lucky enough to have some amazing, positive influences in my church at a young age.

One day, I was asked to introduce myself to the class. I went through the normal explanation, listing my name, favorite color, favorite animals ... then I smiled widely and exclaimed, "Oh, and I know her!" I pointed at my older friend, proud of my accomplishment, as she laughed at my excitement over such a thing.

It was a moment of honor to be claimed by one of the youth kids because you knew their reputation would soon spread to you. The adults that spent time with those youth would begin to invest in you. The activities the big kids were involved in slowly started to include you. Everything the big kids did, you would mirror. I remember constantly thinking, *I want to be just like you.* I didn't realize how many traits of those youth kids I had taken on until recently. Those teens I had looked up to truly had a significant impact on that time of my life.

Recently, I had the privilege of assisting children's church on Sunday morning. It is one of my favorite things to do when I am home. I had grown up quite a bit since that morning in Sunday school. Honestly, I had forgotten ever looking up to those youth kids at all.

That morning, I walked into the children's room to take attendance. I began roll call, giving my best guess at the spelling of each kid's name. To my excitement, I noticed that there was one little boy in attendance whom I had known since he was born. We were very close when I left for college, and I missed him dearly. I couldn't wait to talk to him after class. It had been months since we had last seen each other. He had grown so much! When he called out his name, I could hear the toothy grin in his voice.

I began to write his name down but was surprised to hear an excited, "I know her!" following his roll call. It took me a second to realize he was talking about me. He was so genuinely proud of the fact that he knew me. It still makes me smile when I think about it.

Immediately, it took me back to when I was in his shoes … young, impressionable, and searching for someone to look up to. I remember so clearly how much I craved acceptance and validation from someone I trusted. Now I was grown. Now, I *was* that person. It was a little dizzying when I realized how quickly I had changed from the child to the big kid.

As I thought about this interaction, I questioned whether we still act this way as young adults. Was there someone that I still looked up to? Was there someone I respected so much that I desired to claim her name as part of my *identity*? As these questions swirled around in my head, an incredible scene from Mark 10 came to mind. I imagined children all crowded around Jesus's feet, gleefully exclaiming, "I know Him, I know Him!" With full joy and excitement, they claimed Jesus as part of their identity. I wonder, do we hold that much reverence and respect for

Jesus? We may call ourselves Christians, but do we consider Him a necessary part of the explanation of our identity? Though we may not be children anymore, we are still just as impressionable. We aren't going around seeking a big kid's approval. We have a higher name to boast. We get to claim the name of Jesus.

We are a mess of broken, sinful, and damaged people. Yet, God wants us to claim His name despite our fallen state. He is asking us to exclaim, "I know Him!" to anyone that will listen. What an amazing concept is that? The Creator of the universe wants to be associated with us. He wants to take us under His wings, teach us, guide us, and direct us. In the same way we studied the actions of the big kids growing up, we should be studying the nature of God. Every aspect of our lives should reflect Him. Claim Him as your own. Shout it from the rooftops. Let everyone hear about the one who called you His own.

Jesus said, "Let the little children come to me, and do not hinder them, for the kingdom of heaven belongs to such as these."
—Matthew 19:14 (ESV)

Do not lie to each other, since you have taken off your old self with its practices and have put on the new self, which is being renewed in knowledge in the image of its Creator.
—Colossians 3:9–10 (ESV)

Therefore, if anyone is in Christ, the new creation has come: The old has gone, the new is here!
—2 Corinthians 5:17 (ESV)

PERSONAL REFLECTION QUESTIONS

- What is a story from your life that is similar to the story shared above? How did it make you feel? How did you react to it?

- Who was someone that you looked up to growing up? Why did you want to be like them? What did you change about your life to mirror theirs? Looking back on it now, do you think these were positive or negative changes?

- Is there someone in your life that looks up to you? What habits are you portraying that these children might copy? Are you founded in Scripture, or are you teaching them bad habits? What can you do to start making these habits better? How can you point them to God rather than the habits of the world?

- Who is someone that you look up to today? What traits have they established that make you look up to them? How are you trying to copy these in your own life? Are these habits biblically founded?

- Are you approaching faith with the eyes of a child, or with the stance of an adult? Why? What can you change about your life to help you become more vulnerable in your relationship with Christ?

- What are some things you have learned about yourself and your relationship with God through this story? How can you use this information to help you grow in your faith?

DETOURS

I would love to tell you that I have my life mapped out. I'd love to tell you I am confident in what I chose to study, the activities I am involved in, or that I have some semblance of an idea about my future. But honestly? I have no clue. I don't know where God is leading me right now. When I don't know what I am supposed to be doing, I begin to stress that what I *am* doing isn't God's plan—that despite my constant prayers and conversations with God, I have somehow missed His directions for me. I imagine myself standing at a three-way fork. One path is clearly wrong, but the two remaining paths both appear good. There is no defining marker as to which path is right. There must be one, I just can't tell which path that is. So, because I don't know how God wants me to move forward, I stand frozen in fear, not choosing a path at all.

I figure if I don't move forward, I can't accidentally commit to something I wasn't supposed to. I refuse to move as if eventually I'll hear God's voice booming from heaven telling me what my next move should be. Though that would be amazing, I'm pretty sure that isn't going to happen … ever. So I'm just stuck here, standing still in my uncertainty because I am terrified of straying from the so-called perfect path.

We are convinced that if we follow this path, then we will somehow avoid all heartache or pain. It is as if the path has some magical quality that removes anything unpleasant. We have been told that when things go wrong it is because we made a bad decision somewhere along the road and our poor choice took us off the path. Now we are lost, confused, and unsure of how to get back. This concept has taken a hold of our minds and paralyzed many of us with fear. It is a belief that is incredibly toxic.

We cannot continue to believe that there is a perfect life path or that all detours are bad. These ideas are destroying our mental and spiritual health. If we continue to evaluate our life choices based on this perfect road, we are never going to move forward. We are going to stand at that fork in the road, never being able to decide on what path to follow. Sometimes, choices merely lead you down different detours that end up in the same location. If you are actively seeking God's will, you are not going to end up outside of His plan for you. However, you cannot stand still, frozen in fear of accidentally straying off this perfect path. You have to move.

If both options seem beneficial, and neither option is contradictory to the Bible, you are likely approaching a detour. Yes, the experiences will be different for the separate paths. You will likely learn different lessons, meet different people, and do different activities. But, if you are pursuing Christ, both detours will end up at the destination of His perfect will for you—you'll just learn different lessons along the way. Stop fearing the unknown. Life is full of detours. They must be accepted and embraced in order to learn from them.

God gives us free will for a reason. We must be allowed to continue to choose Him and to form a life of our own. This means that we are given choices, or forks in the road, throughout life. Do not be afraid of falling off the perfect path. There isn't one. There is, however, a perfect God whom you can trust. If you follow Him, you will reach the destination of His will for you. Embrace your detours. He designed them just for you.

The Lord makes firm the steps of the one who delights in Him.
—Psalm 37:23 (ESV)

Your word is a lamp for my feet, a light on my path.
—Psalm 119:105 (ESV)

Trust in the Lord with all your heart and lean not on your own understanding; in all your ways submit to him, and he will make your paths straight.
—Proverbs 3:5–6 (ESV)

The Lord works out everything to its proper end—even the wicked for a day of disaster.
—Proverbs 16:4 (ESV)

PERSONAL REFLECTION QUESTIONS

> What is a story from your life that is similar to the story shared above? How did it make you feel? How did you react to it?
> What is a recent fork in the road that you've dealt with? How did you decide to move forward? Why? Was this done with prayer and spiritual guidance, or did you make decisions based on your own wants?
> Describe a time when God led you on a detour in life. Did you get (or are you going) where you wanted to go? Is where you ended better than you expected? What lessons did you learn along the way?

- What is a situation in your life right now where you wish God would just yell out the answer from heaven? Since this (probably) isn't going to happen, what can you do to work closer to finding the answers? Who could pray with you about it?
- What have you been told is the perfect path for your life? Do you agree with this? Who told you this? Is this a person you can trust? Have you compared it with what you believe God's will is for you? Are the things you are pursuing with His will in mind, or society's path to fake success?
- What are some things you have learned about yourself and your relationship with God through this story? How can you use this information to help you grow in your faith?

"WHERE THE LOST THINGS GO"
-A STORY

Author's note: *This is a story of hope. When you go through spiritual valleys, know that you are not alone. We all experience these trials from time to time. During these valleys, it is often hard to see a way out. When hope seems fleeting, God will send someone to remind you of His love for you. Remember that He will always pull you through to the other side. This story is a little bit longer, so grab a blanket, get cozy, and enjoy the read.*

The sunlight beaming through the window, the warm, delicious smell of morning coffee, and the lush feeling of Elise's favorite blanket were her morning routine surroundings. She used to look forward to bright, sunny days, but recently she was doing all she could to avoid them. Why? Because this morning routine wasn't solely sunshine, great coffee, and fluffy blankets; she did her devotionals at this time too. Devotionals used to be her favorite part of the day. She used to love diving into the scriptures and soaking up every word. Now, she read them with disgust, anger, and disbelief.

Painful memories and heartbreak accompanied most of her days. She lived in fear of the future, dreading each sunrise.

Negativity and stress had become her closest companions. Every attempt to escape the prison in her mind merely brought her more confusion and uncertainty. She had tried. She had failed. She had given up.

A lot has happened within the past few months, she thought. *If I want to take a break from God, I am entitled to it. I just need some time to sort through life without Him. I don't think He caused this hurt, but I can't get the thought out of my mind that He allowed it. I don't understand and I am taking a well-deserved break.*

She looked down at her open Bible and her eyes caught a verse, Psalm 46:10. She began to read. "Be still, and know that I am God." Laughing, she stopped reading as thoughts of stress and busyness flooded her mind.

"If I become still, I will never finish my day's work. I have too much to do to allow time for rest."

She gently closed her Bible and set it up on her bookshelf. It was time to open up shop. Her parents were away on a small vacation and left the shop for her to take care of this week. Not that her parents worked the shop often, they were so busy they rarely had time for it. Honestly, they didn't even have that much time for her. She spent most days by herself or at work. Luckily, the trip to work wasn't very far. Taking a trip down the stairs was an easy commute. Plus, she had always adored looking through the many rows of dusty shelves when she arrived. They were full of other people's trash, soon to become another's treasure. It fit the name perfectly: Where the Lost Things Go.

Looking at the time, she decided she should probably crawl out of bed. She threw her hair into a messy bun, grabbed her coffee mug, and shuffled downstairs to open the windows and turn the *closed* sign around. The day had officially begun. She glanced at her watch and counted thirteen more hours until close. This was going to be a long day.

About an hour after opening, a sweet-looking old woman stumbled in with her husband. They must have been a striking couple in their youth, for even now they seemed to radiate love and happiness.

I will never find that, she thought grumpily. *I will be a lonely, crazy cat lady for the rest of my days. Better to accept it now, I suppose.*

"Ahem!" The old lady coughed.

Thrown out of her pity party, Elise realized she had been ignoring her customers. The old woman had been trying to get her attention, and she hadn't even noticed.

"Oh my goodness, I'm so sorry. Um, welcome to Where the Lost Things Go. Can I help you find anything?" Elise asked.

"Well," the woman began, "I am looking for a small trinket to get my granddaughter for her birthday. Maybe a piece of jewelry … coffee cup … book … anything, really."

"Hmmm, let me see. Oh! Over here we have some jewelry. Maybe something in here might work?"

The old woman walked over to the jewelry stand and pulled out a silver ring covered in dust and dirt.

Barely having the ability to make out the mound of filth as a ring, Elise decided she had better clean it up for her customer. "Oh goodness, let me clean that up for you. I don't have anything fancy, but I am sure soap and water could do wonders." Elise winked.

"Oh, yes, please! I have a feeling this ring is quite beautiful beneath all that. I would like to see what it truly looks like."

As the caked-on dirt fell into the sink, the true identity of the ring began to unfold. A small opal rested between two diamonds, set neatly on either side of this ornate piece of jewelry. Long, curly details within the silver made this ring a wonder to behold. Elise had never seen it before. The ring was tiny and dirty; there was no reason to bother with it before now. She realized then the steal this woman had come upon.

"That is stunning, Mrs.—"

"Tendresse," the woman completed with a smile.

"Well, Mrs. Tendresse, I am sure your granddaughter will adore that!"

"Yes." She smiled. "It is quite beautiful. But I would like to find one more thing for her."

Elise couldn't stop looking at the ring … it reminded her of her grandmother's. How she missed her. She would have bought that ring for herself had she seen it before. Now it was too late.

Should've paid more attention! she scolded herself.

After a few minutes of perusing the store, Mrs. Tendresse approached the counter with an eclectic book of poetry and the coveted ring. Looking around, she asked, "Do you usually run this store by yourself? Seems a little lonely, just you and these misfit objects. What do you do for fun around here, my dear?"

"Fun?" Elise laughed, incredulously. "I don't really have time for that. My parents are often away, so yes, it is usually just me and the shop. I enjoy helping my family, but it can get stressful at times. I'm under a lot of pressure. I don't sleep much and it feels like all I do is work. I really wish I could leave this all behind and just exist. I'm sick of it all."

Wow, overshare much? Elise sighed, "You definitely didn't ask for any of that. I am so sorry … just ignore me. I am having a bit of a rough day today."

Mrs. Tendresse smiled kindly. "No worries, love. May I give you some advice?"

"I suppose so."

"Never forget who holds each day. Do you think it is you that raises the sun each morning? Are you sending the wind? Are you lighting the stars at night? No. We couldn't possibly do that. In the same way, we cannot possibly balance everything in our life by ourselves. The weight of the world is crushing. Trying to carry it alone on your shoulders will only cause you to stumble and fall. You are a fine young lady, Miss Elise. Let Him take this burden from you. You don't need to figure this out alone. Let Him hold your hand and walk the road with you."

Quietly, Mrs. Tendresse exited the store. Her husband had gone earlier to wait in the car so that he could listen to the ball game. The Tendresses drove off, and Elise was left standing alone and confused.

She knew what the woman had said was true. Yet it seemed as if Elise was just another item in her store of lost things. She slowly walked around her store, searching for answers to an unknown question. As she passed a bookshelf, she saw an old, dusty, leather-bound Bible.

Opening it, she turned to where she knew she would find reassurance. She read, "Isaiah 41:10: 'So do not fear, for I am with you; do not be dismayed, for I am your God. I will strengthen you and help you; I will uphold you with my righteous right hand.'"

Tears fell as these words washed over her soul. She remembered how she used to rely on God, how when bad things were happening it was easy to let Him lead. Now? Life was harder than ever; she shut God out of her life, and she was alone and helpless. She didn't want God; she wanted to handle it all on her own. The truth, however, was painfully clear. She could not do it alone. She had no ability to pull herself out of the mire she climbed into, no ability to shed light into the darkness. She knew she could not continue this way.

Tears flooded her cheeks as realizations hit her like bullets to the heart, breaking down each and every wall she had been building. She sank to the floor and hugged her sweater around her tightly.

"God, if you can still hear me, I am so, so sorry. I want to be the leader of my own life, but I can't do it. I'm drowning. I need you to hold my hand and guide me. I need you back, Lord."

Wiping the tears from her eyes, she stood up and returned to the counter. "I bet that sweet old woman doesn't even know the impact she had on me today." She laughed to herself. "I hope her granddaughter likes her ring. I know I would ..."

Walking back upstairs, she grabbed the Bible she had neglected only hours before, turned to the journal section in the back, and made a quick entry entitled "The Day the Lost Thing was Found." Happily, she closed her Bible and headed back downstairs.

Ten hours left, she thought. This time, that thought didn't fill her with dread. Now she was ready to face her life with the energy and vigor she had so long been missing. It was a good feeling.

*

Two weeks later.

Glancing at her clock, Elise realized she had run long on her devotion time again and was late to open up the shop. Grabbing her coffee, she took a sip and gave a quick morning prayer. "Thanks for the sunshine this morning. It's beautiful today. Please help the store have a good day, and for all my family and friends to stay happy and safe. Love you. Amen."

She waltzed back downstairs to the shop, opened the windows, flipped the sign, and propped open the door to let some fresh air in. It wasn't super busy today, fairly slow actually. Around 1:30 a car pulled up. Just then, the phone rang. Elise ran back to answer the call.

When she came back out, Elise was met with the kind face of Mrs. Tendresse. "Mrs. Tendresse! What can I help you with? Did your granddaughter like her gifts? How are you?" Elise inquired with a smile.

"Well!" She laughed. "You seem in a much better spirit than last I saw you, Miss Elise. Actually, it turned out that this ring was the wrong size ... and I remember a distinct look of longing on your face the last time you saw it. I was going to sell it, but I wanted an excuse to check in on my favorite antique shop worker."

"Umm, how many antique stores do you shop at, Mrs. Tendresse?"

"Just this one," she commented slyly. "It seems from your high spirits that you might have taken my advice."

"Honestly? I feel amazing. I still have rough days, but I've learned that's OK. God is with us even in ... well, *especially* in the hard times. Your advice was much needed, and I have been wanting to see you for some time to thank you. So … thank you …" Elise finished awkwardly.

"I am so happy to hear that! I can see that you mean it, too. Those aren't just words. That message is coming right from your soul. Elise, I would like to give you this ring. I want it to be a physical reminder that you are not walking alone. Remember that we all go through phases of good and bad times. Much like this ring began as a beautiful creation, was marred, then purified and given a second life, you, Elise, have been chosen, purified, and given a new life. Shine the way you were made to—uniquely, brilliantly, and beautifully."

Mrs. Tendresse pulled the ring out of a velvet satchel and slid it onto Elise's finger. It was a perfect fit. "Beautiful!" Mrs. Tendresse concluded, clasping her hands in excitement. "Now," she sighed, "I assume my dear husband is still waiting in the car as I ramble on. I must be leaving. Goodbye, Elise. I hope you have a wonderful day."

"Th-thank you." Elise stuttered. "I'm at a loss for words."

"Then there's no need to speak!" she winked. "Enjoy your day, Elise." With that, she was gone.

Elise looked down at her new—or old?—exquisite piece of jewelry. A newfound peace washed over her as she quietly whispered, "Lord, you know my heart. May You never let me forget what You have done for me. There is never a moment You have not cared for or loved me. There was never a moment You were not beside me. Your love is a gift I don't understand, one I could never deserve … yet You give it willingly. All I can say is thank you for finding me and seeing the beauty hidden by sin. Thank You for making me shine for You once again. Amen."

As the fresh spring air tickled her face and the sunshine warmed her soul, the ring glittered like a thousand stars. She was whole again. It was time to continue her journey, but this time she knew she wouldn't be alone. He was with her. He always had been.

PERSONAL REFLECTION QUESTIONS

- What is a story from your life that is similar to the story shared above? How did it make you feel? How did you react to it?

- Have you been through a time like Elise's when spending time with God just felt heavy? What was happening in your life that made you feel this way? Is it still like that now? What steps can you take to start fixing this situation?

- Do you struggle with extreme independence? Why do you think this is the case? What can you do to remind yourself that you aren't walking alone?

- Do you feel overwhelmed by the weight of the world's expectations? What expectations do you feel right now?

- How are you focusing on pursuing Christ rather than the world? What could you improve on?

- What are some things you have learned about yourself and your relationship with God through this story? How can you use this information to help you grow in your faith?

Printed in the United States
by Baker & Taylor Publisher Services